RECALLING OUR OWN STORIES

RECALLING OUR OWN STORIES

Spiritual Renewal for Religious Caregivers

Edward P. Wimberly

Jossey-Bass Publishers
San Francisco

Substantial discounts on bulk quantities of Jossey-Bass
books are available to corporations, professional
associations, and other organizations. For details
and discount information, contact the special sales
department at (415) 433-1740; Fax (800) 605-2665.

Jossey-Bass Web address: http://www.josseybass.com

 Manufactured in the United States of America on Lyons
Falls Turin Book. This paper is acid-free and 100 percent
totally chlorine-free.

Library of Congress Cataloging-in-Publication Data

Wimberly, Edward P., date.
    Recalling our own stories : spiritual renewal for religious
caregivers / Edward P. Wimberly. —1st ed.
        p. cm. — (The Jossey-Bass religion-in-practice series)
    Includes bibliographical references and index.
    ISBN 0-7879-0363-9 (alk. paper)
        1. Clergy—Psychology. 2. Clergy—Religious life. 3. Church
work—Psychological aspects. 4. Pastoral theology. I. Title.
II. Series.
BV4398.W56 1997
248.8'9—dc21   96-51202

FIRST EDITION

PB Printing 10 9 8 7 6 5 4 3 2

The Jossey-Bass
Religion-in-Practice Series

CONTENTS

To my brother, Edgar Van Wimberly Jr.,
November 15, 1942–February 16, 1996

PREFACE

FOR SOME YEARS NOW, I have been doing spiritual renewal retreats seeking to help fellow ministers and religious caregivers explore our deep convictions and beliefs about ourselves, our marriages, our families, and our lives in ministry. Over time, I noticed that the problems that people brought to the retreats seemed to cluster in certain patterns. There are themes, deeply rooted and ingrained, that appear to inform everything we do in our lives. I found that a particular concept of *mythology* helped me to bring meaning to the patterns emerging from our lives. Eventually, I identified and named these themes.

As the retreats continued, participants began to ask if the ideas and insights I was developing had been published. My answer was to review some of the literature that exists around the themes I was identifying. However, I did not find any works that approached retreats and spiritual renewal in the same way as I did. The participants' quest for more information about my specific approach sparked my interest in publishing what I was trying to do in the workshops and retreats I was leading.

As I thought about writing this book, certain personal cases came to mind that I had encountered in the retreats. In recalling the specifics of those cases, I made connections to still others in the retreats, classes, and counseling that I was doing. As a result, this book is about the many people whose lives have had a great impact on me. I have protected their identities by giving them fictitious names and changing key data.

I intend the insights drawn from these cases to help us clergy and religious caregivers face the specific challenges we encounter in ministry. The ideas are also meant to assist the practitioners among us who work with clergy and caregivers to be more helpful as we seek to facilitate their meeting these challenges.

To this end, this book has three purposes. First, because we religious and professional caregivers are powerfully influenced by cultural expectations that we will show superheroic empathy in our personal and professional lives, this book is designed to enable caregivers to map out and come to grips with those influences. Second, the book helps us explore and edit, and thus reauthor, the personal, marital, family, and ministerial mythologies that make up our image of self, our attitudes toward inter-action with others, our expectations regarding performance and role, and our convictions about ministry. Such exploration and reauthoring enables us to be more human, and to use our own healed inadequacies as sources of strength for ministry and caregiving. Third, the book is intended to pro-vide a model for spiritual and emotional renewal grounded in narrative psychological and spiritual approaches.

Several assumptions undergird these purposes. First, human experience must have meaning; it can be "storied" or arranged in sequences that give a coherent account to that experience (White and Epston, 1990). This account is called a story, self-narrative, or mythology. Second, these stories, narratives, and mythologies not only give coherent accounts of personal experience but also help give meaning to marital, family, and caregiving life. Third, such stories or myths are made up of ideal images of what it means to be a self, what it means to be married and live in a family, and what it means to be a caregiver in ministry. Fourth, these storied experi-ences are real in the sense that they shape our lives and relationships (White and Epston, 1990). Fifth, these myths are often destructive of the growth and well-being of the self and others; and therefore, they need to be reau-thored to return growth and life to us. Sixth, gender, racial, and religious cultural factors help these myths take shape in our lives; and these influ-ences need to be identified and explored when indicated.

Contribution

Currently, books exist that help the caregiving practitioner examine the role of narratives in the life of the counselee or those in need of therapeutic assis-tance. However, very little literature deals with the role of narratives and sto-ried experiences in the caregiver's life and the impact of story on the process of caregiving. This book offers a new way to bring narrative theory to the religious and professional caregiver's understanding of the ideal images of caregiving, ministry, the self, and the self in relationship to others. These ideal images shape our experiences; therefore, the book seeks to strongly connect the ministry of caregiving, cultural expectations around caregiv-ing, and the sense of self (both personal and in relationship to others).

Audience

This book addresses professionals whose caregiving is primarily religious: ordained ministers, rabbis, religious counselors, lay religious counselors, and students in undergraduate and graduate professional caregiving programs holding a religious point of view.

I intend this book to be for a multicultural audience. The case studies are of caregivers from different cultural backgrounds: Euro-American, African American, and Hispanic American. It can be used in any class in undergraduate and graduate courses in religious counseling. It is particularly suited to seminary courses in pastoral counseling.

Outline of Contents

The book is organized to address specific issues that religious and professional caregivers face in four types of mythology: personal, marital, family, and ministry. Vignettes and case studies in each chapter set the stage for understanding those problematic mythologies in the caregiver's life and ministry that need to be reauthored. I present a model of reauthoring and show how it is done in particular case studies.

Chapter One introduces a narrative approach to spiritual renewal grounded in biblical and church tradition. Chapter Two presents common, basic, personal myths that I have encountered repeatedly in retreats, classes, and counseling. Chapter Three identifies frequent myths in family and marriage, and Chapter Four names typical examples of ministerial myths. Chapters Two through Four end with exercises meant to ease you into your journey by reflecting on what these myths mean in your own life.

Chapter Five outlines the reauthoring process; we look at its various phases in brief vignettes. Then Chapters Six through Nine present in detail case studies that illustrate how the reauthoring process actually worked in the lives of specific people. The final chapter proposes steps you can take as you return to the exercises that were presented at the end of Chapters Two through Four and analyze the answers. Chapter Ten also presents ideas for further exploration of the themes affecting spiritual replenishment in religious caregiving; it also gives information as to how we can enlist the aid of others in reauthoring our own myths.

Acknowledgments

For a number of years, the Interdenominational Theological Center, under the leadership of its president James Costen, provided faculty development funds for research leading to publication. I am deeply indebted to the generosity of the ITC for supporting the research in this book. I am also indebted to the many students and workshop participants who so graciously consented to have their stories told in this book. Students in the courses Pastoral Care and Inner Healing and Foundations for Ministry need special recognition. My sister-in-law, Margaret Wimberly, did outstanding work editing this book.

Atlanta, Georgia   Edward P. Wimberly
February 1997

THE AUTHOR

EDWARD P. WIMBERLY is Jarena Lee Professor of Pastoral Care and Counseling at the Interdenominational Theological Center (ITC), Atlanta, where he also heads the Thomas J. Pugh Pastoral Counseling Center. He has been an ordained minister of the United Methodist church since 1969 and has served pastorates in Winchendon and Worcester, Massachusetts. In addition to his work at the ITC, he has served on the faculties of the Garrett-Evangelical Theological Seminary in Evanston, Illinois, and Oral Roberts University School of Theology in Tulsa, Oklahoma. He received his B.A. degree (1965) in history from the University of Arizona, Tucson, and both the bachelor of sacred theology (1968) and the master of sacred theology (1971), with a major in the sociology of religion, from the Boston University School of Theology. He completed his Ph.D. degree (1976) at the Boston University Graduate School, Division of Theological Studies, in the areas of pastoral psychology and counseling. Among his many publications on pastoral counseling are *Prayer in Pastoral Counseling* (1990), *African American Pastoral Care* (1991), *Using Scripture in Pastoral Counseling* (1994), and *Counseling African American Couples and Families* (1997).

RECALLING OUR OWN STORIES

TO BE CALLED ANEW

FINDING SPIRITUAL REPLENISHMENT
IN OUR OWN STORIES

I HAVE BEEN ASKED to do a number of spiritual renewal retreats. Those of us who are engaged in caring for others who are in ministry have seen firsthand how people need spiritual replenishment in their professions. The need is ongoing because many of us regularly feel we are running out of energy and gas. More than once, we have faced burnout. I believe we have all felt the need to refuel, to tap the sources of renewal that reside in our faith community.

Original Motivation: Our Call

In seeking spiritual renewal, we can take up the neglected tradition of reconnecting with our original motivation for ministry. In the Judeo-Christian tradition, that motivation is often referred to as "the call"; it was our first awareness that a form of ministry would be our life's work. Generally, most of us in ministry can identify the point in our lives at which we can say we made a commitment to ministry. Some of us came to our call after a period of growth and development in which we came to recognize our own gifts of ministry, gifts that others might have recognized, confirmed, and affirmed for us. Some of us had a more dramatic call: something sensational happened to bring our calling abruptly to awareness. Whether our awareness came suddenly or over time, a chance to reconnect with our original call is often the beginning of spiritual renewal.

As a boy, I learned from my dad how he went about finding renewal and meaning in life. He is a retired African American minister in the Methodist tradition. Once a year or so, he would rehearse from the pulpit his call to ministry. I can't say at what point in his life's journey I first heard him tell his story, but I do remember several things from hearing those rehearsals.

First, he would tell how he had finished a black college and returned to his home in Florida to teach. This was in the early 1930s, a time of full segregation. Before my father left Lincoln University in Oxford, Pennsylvania, one of the administrators recognized his proclivity for ministry; Dad had not seen it. The administrator told him that he could have a scholarship to seminary if he decided to enter the ministry. My dad thanked the administrator for his kind and generous offer but said he was not ready for such an endeavor at that time in his life.

Dad taught school for several years. Then, to his surprise, what the college administrator discerned several years earlier began to manifest itself. One uneventful evening, he lay sprawled across his bed, not anticipating anything but sleep since he was very tired from a long day's work at school. He was not asleep; he was in a semiwakened state. Suddenly a vision appeared that would alter his life. Dad's voice would grow excited every time he retold what transpired. He vividly saw himself in front of a congregation, preaching the gospel. A small group of people were sitting before him, on the stairs on which he was standing. He slowly moved backwards up the stairs while he expounded on the word of God. When he reached the top of the stairs, the vision disappeared as suddenly as it had come.

My dad attributed religious significance to the vision; it was his call to ministry. He knew, he said, that he had to begin preparing himself for a new life's work. Instantly, the college administrator's offer of several years earlier came to mind. The next morning, Dad contacted the administrator and discovered that the invitation and scholarship to seminary remained open. He made plans to attend seminary the following autumn.

The second thing I remember about my dad's rehearsal of his call was that for him it was a form of spiritual renewal. It appeared to bring a new perspective to his life. Of course, this is my conclusion looking retrospectively on what I saw on those occasions. No doubt he intended his testimony to contribute to the growth and development of his audience. But he seemed to derive new meaning for his own life from his excursus back to his original call.

One reason I so boldly interpret the effect of his rehearsing the call relates to what he often said following his recitation. He would use another story to interpret his call. In Acts 25:13–26:32, Paul defended himself after being arrested by telling King Agrippa the story of his own call on the Damascus Road. My father would recount the story of Paul's testimony, concluding with Paul's famous words in Acts 26:19, "Where-for, O King Agrippa, I was not disobedient to the heavenly vision" (Note: throughout this book all citations are from *The New Oxford Annotated Bible,* edited in 1977 by May and Metzger). I conclude from what my dad offered in interpretation that he drew some measure of focus and new life from recounting the two stories.

Paul found himself in hostile circumstances, as did many of the Christians in the early church. He periodically derived a sense of renewal from returning to his reasons for arriving in the predicament. Likewise, I surmise that my dad found similar renewal for his ministry by also returning to his memory of his own call.

From my dad and from this episode in the life of Paul, I conclude that a model of spiritual renewal exists in Scripture. It is many centuries old, but it informs what is needed in spiritual renewal today. Such a model helps us as religious caregivers to return routinely to our original motivation for ministry as a means of renewal. The model of spiritual renewal that I point to comes from African American spirituality, which has a strongly biblical character (Phelps, 1990). It also has a dimension of confession and self-disclosure to it (Myers, 1994). Telling stories about one's call to ministry dates back to the slave narrative tradition (Wimberly and Wimberly, 1986). This tradition of spirituality has shaped both my father's and my own way of doing and conceptualizing spirituality.

I have found that this biblical tradition of spiritual renewal appeals to more than just African American religious caregivers. I have used it for many years with different ethnic and racial groups; they have all found it helpful and timely in their own spiritual renewal. It is one among many approaches to renewing the vitality of our ministry.

A third thing I learned about spiritual renewal from my father is that it requires not only reflecting on the call but also rehearsing and recounting the story in a community or public setting. My dad chose the pulpit, and Paul had to use the courtroom. Spiritual renewal is greatly enhanced when it is done with others present.

Reviewing our call in a community of caring people, especially a community of colleagues, has much significance. Time out with colleagues, as in a retreat from the daily routines of ministry, enhances the quality of spiritual renewal. When we use this particular model in the presence of many, we are grateful not to be alone in the wilderness of ministry. We feel less vulnerable to isolation and are encouraged to risk more of ourselves in the process. I hear people report that the companionship gives them courage to face the edge of their personal growth that would be hard to face alone. Some have found that this form of group spiritual renewal hastens emotional and interpersonal maturity along with spiritual renewal.

Renewing our motivation by reconnecting to our original call allows us to visualize again how God has decisively acted in our lives at crucial junctures. It reminds us that God has been intricately involved in our lives. The routine duties of ministry and life take on new meaning when looked at in light of the call.

But spiritual renewal involves more than returning to our original motivation for entering ministry. It also examines past and present experiences and issues in our lives that are related to ministry. For example, recovery from burnout—or its extreme case, a sudden and public "flameout," as some call it—involves recalling our motivation for entering the ministry and examining the issues of burnout in light of our call. The call is a marker event that we must return to periodically to examine where we are in life, and to alter our way of believing and doing.

Spiritual renewal is finding a fresh, novel, and creative way of allowing the call to reorient our present lives so as to bring replenishment and hope. Spiritual renewal is a process of connecting with our original motivation for ministry, and then moving systematically into examining areas of our lives in light of that call.

Mythology

In the spiritual renewal process that I propose in this book, the concept of mythology is immensely helpful. By *mythology,* I mean *the beliefs and convictions that people have about themselves, their relationships with others, their roles in life, and their ministry.* As used here, myth refers to the way beliefs and convictions are constructed and how these constructions shape our lives and our behavior.

Beliefs and convictions are represented by certain repetitive themes that appear in the stories we tell. At times, I may use the words *myth* and *theme* synonymously, although they are different. Myths are the stories we tell, while themes reflect the beliefs and convictions in the stories.

The Project of Existence

The call constitutes the "project of existence" (Van Kaam, 1964, p. 20). The project of existence is an overarching framework in an individual's life that gives meaning and shape to everything that goes on. It is a vocational umbrella, or window, through which we look at all of what we do. It is the dominant, self-understood purpose for which we have been born. It tells us what to do daily in our ministry, and it informs how we execute our roles and functions. It serves as a kind of road map in fulfilling our call.

Narrative Story

Supporting this project of existence is a worldview, or narrative story, that gives shape and meaning to the roles we execute in ministry. It "relates" (in the sense of telling) to us what our role is. We find in our lives a dominant story or myth out of which we come, while the other stories or myths in our lives become submyths or secondary myths. The dominant myth, the project of existence, gives meaning and shape to our lives. For example, one person's dominant story may be that she is always an embattled hero working valiantly against great odds, while another's dominant story may be one of awe and gratitude in the face of surprising gifts over which he has little instrumental control.

The project of existence has at its core the call coming from God. For my father and the apostle Paul, renewal came because the source of the call was outside themselves. God provided the call, the power to fulfill the call, and the historic meaning for the call. What people who are called have done historically, then, is orient themselves and their personality, relationships, and ministry in terms of the call from God. Spiritual renewal is a reorientation process of allowing the original call and its ongoing nature to continually transform our lives in the present.

A basic assumption in spiritual renewal is that the call is ongoing. Consequently, the project of existence—the dominant story of our lives—is being renewed by God each day. Connecting with this transcendent activity brings renewal into our lives.

The Problem of Submyths

Lesser stories—our submyths—often take center stage in our lives. When this happens, we suffer loss of meaning and direction. The submyths or lesser myths of our lives emerge from our experiences as human beings. They function best when they are in line with our project of existence or our call, when they are being renewed daily by the ongoing call of our lives. However, sometimes the submyths of our lives are so powerful that they block the influence of the ongoing call.

When the lesser myths block the working of the call in our lives, spiritual renewal becomes the removing of the blocks that are in the way of our call. Spiritual renewal is an attempt to bring our submyths back in line with the ongoing call or project of existence. Consequently, it is important to identify the submyths at work in our lives and bring them into connection with the ongoing call in our lives.

The Problem of Perfection

One of the lesser myths that block the call in our lives is the cultural myth of "perfection." The myth of perfection relates to the domination of the therapeutic model that greatly influences ministry today.

Since the turn of the century, a psychological model has been at the center of our understanding of the pastor's relationship with parishioners (Hollifield, 1983). In some minds, the increasing influence of psychology and counseling psychology has secularized pastoral conversation. That is, psychological language has slowly replaced religious language in pastoral dialogue during this century.

Empathy

A major theme in much of our pastoral conversation today is the perfection of empathy. In the history of modern pastoral counseling, for example, empathy was not seen as just a skill. Rather, it was a way of approaching life and caring that yielded an engaged stance, a relational posture, where human beings connected with each other (Clinebell, 1984). Growing out of the humanistic philosophical tradition, empathy entails several assumptions: human beings are innately good and worthwhile; they tend toward actualizing themselves by unfolding from within; their growth comes from evolving and interacting; human relationships are essential to the unfolding of human possibilities; and empathy, or entering into another's internal world, is essential to a person's growth, development, and self-actualization (Hunter, 1990). Thus empathy became a comprehensive perspective for viewing all human relationships, and for viewing what all human beings needed to become true persons. Empathy became all-encompassing for the pastoral counseling movement and has continued to influence the way pastors have been trained since the 1940s. The ability to be empathic has thus been considered the most critical element for effective caregiving. It has achieved the level of a practical mythology as a theme that is centrally emphasized in pastoral relationships.

In the myth of empathy, it is possible to achieve perfect empathy or reach complete positive regard for another person, without flaw. Entering another's internal frame of reference and viewing the world through his or her eyes is not only achievable but perfectible. To be perfect in demonstrating empathy means the caregiver takes on the other's point of view so completely that the caregiver's own interests, attitudes, concerns, and problems are prevented from interfering with those of the other person. In general, textbooks in pastoral care assume this expectation of achieving complete empathy. The result is that many pastoral counselors enter counseling relationships believing that it is possible to achieve self-sacrificing empathy.

Carrie Doehring, the author of *Taking Care: Monitoring Power Dynamics and Relational Boundaries in Pastoral Care and Counseling,* talks about the social context of the perfection of empathy: "In a culture in which attunement may be greatly lacking in many relational contexts (in the community, in work relationships, and in the corporate world) there may be a demand for 'perfect attunement' in dyadic healing and nurturing relationships. The parent, the minister, the counselor, or the teacher is expected to be an expert at attunement and empathy" (Doehring, 1995, p. 80).

The emphasis on perfection has led people to describe the effort to achieve empathy as having "sucked the life out of the caregiver," and as having "the potential to contaminate" us as caregivers if we have no place to turn to for emotional and spiritual renewal. How to renew and sustain our vital spiritual and emotional life as religious and professional caregivers, and thus replenish our energy, remains a crucial need in the face of the demand for perfect empathy.

The myth of perfection dominates North American professional circles in caregiving. Beneath this myth is a superheroic narrative; it supports the caregiver's effort to sacrifice self regardless of whether that self is regularly renewed or not (Messer, 1989; Jewett, 1993; Passmore, 1970; Fenn, 1987; Jewett and Lawrence, 1988). The theme that supports the notion of perfection is that we caregiving practitioners desire and expect to be flawless in connecting empathically with those needing our care. The theme also implies that we be free from personal hang-ups, and perfectly available and approachable for the person in need of care. It calls for denial and repression of our humanness: "To achieve perfection in any of its classical senses, as so many perfectibilists have admitted, it would first be necessary to cease to be human, to become godlike, to rise above the human condition. But a god knows nothing of love, or science, or art, or craft, of family and friends, of discovery, of pride in work" (Passmore, 1970, p. 326).

To be a superheroic empathizer, we must deny all aspects of our own humanness. Doing so cuts us off from the human family. It also leads to us to deny our own needs for spiritual, emotional, and interpersonal renewal. It sets the stage for burnout and failure in ministry. It makes us vulnerable. As Doehring points out, it leads to neglecting ourselves as well as those for whom we care—especially when we lack the expertise we need to carry out empathy well (Doehring, 1995).

"Good Enough" Empathy

Our expectation of achieving perfect empathy is unreasonable. It is unrealistic to expect that we can execute empathy without flaw. But it *is* realistic to expect from us "good enough" empathy. Good enough empathy is not flawless. Good enough empathy is rooted in an awareness that although we are wounded and hurting, we have taken time to tend to the wounds. Healing our own wounds means they can be a source of healing for those whose wounds are similar to ours. Good enough empathy means we have had our wounds transformed from sources of personal weakness to reservoirs of strength for those in need. This presupposes that we spend time in spiritual renewal, time in spiritual retreat.

Throughout this book, I draw a subtle contrast between realism and perfection. *Perfection* refers to flawless performance. *Realism* refers to performance that is permeated with a grace-filled acceptance of our limitations and flaws (and our strengths). Grace-filled realism enables us to make significant—but not unflawed—contributions to the lives of others. It is not driven by fear of falling short of an impossible external standard, or law, or expectation. Rather, grace-filled realism is caregiving nurtured by a transcendent love that motivates and energizes.

A Case of Disappointed Perfection

It is not easy for religious caregivers to move beyond the perfectionistic impulse to awareness of the need for spiritual renewal and retreat. Perfectionistic thinking is so strong that we deny our own need for healing and resist the efforts of others to help us see our vulnerability and suffering.

I met a pastor at the grocery store. He had just left a group of other pastors in a hospital, engaging in what is called clinical pastoral education (CPE, an interpersonal training program for ministers and chaplains located primarily in hospitals).

The pastor looked very tired, and somewhat perplexed. He sighed: "I wish someone had warned me about this CPE. I'm tired. I have four weeks to go. I get so tired of discovering how many inadequacies I have. It's embarrassing for others to see just how inadequate I am. I try to hide my vulnerabilities, but others find them out. I wish they would give me some breathing space."

Part of this minister's self-expectation was perfection. Rather than seeing CPE as an opportunity to grow and improve his interpersonal skills for ministry, he wanted the CPE experience to affirm his perfect ministerial skills. He was so tired because he was expending so much effort trying to keep his imperfections hidden from himself and others.

This illustration is typical of many who experience CPE. The myth of perfection dominates; it is hard for us to consider becoming wounded healers. Some of us feel that our call to ministry bestowed upon us all the gifts and graces needed for ministry, and therefore training is not required. CPE helps us ministers get in touch with our vulnerabilities so we can learn to care for ourselves and our own needs.

Transformation of the Walking Wounded

The myth of perfection has engendered many other metaphors and myths about ministry. For example, Henri Nouwen coined the metaphor of the "wounded healer" as a response to the perfectionistic myth (Nouwen, 1972; Messer, 1989). Rather than deny our wounds and vulnerability, Nouwen emphasized the need to embrace one's woundedness and tend to it by seeking spiritual direction and therapy.

A colleague of mine, Calvin Morris, offered the metaphor "walking wounded" as another reply to the perfectionistic myth. He uses the term to characterize those of us who deny our vulnerability and woundedness and who, consequently, walk around as wounded people seeking to help others. Instead of achieving good enough empathy, we become dangerous to ourselves and to those we seek to care for. We cannot temporarily set our own needs aside or keep them out of the way in our caring effort. Sometimes, as walking wounded, we use our caring relationships to *receive* care ourselves by reversing roles with those who are actually in need of pastoral conversation.

Early in my own ministry, I often shared stories from my life that I thought would help my parishioners while I was counseling them. Ordinarily, this would work. But there was one elderly woman with whom I would share my stories—and she would inevitably end up ministering to me! She sensed that I was new in ministry and that I needed motherly attention. Although she had her own needs as well, in our conversations I found myself sharing more from my life and connecting less with her needs.

I began training for pastoral counseling very early in my ministry. In the training, I presented cases to a consultant, who identified my tendency to take the focus away from my counselee. He suggested that I go into therapy for myself and not use my counselees to receive counseling. I was one of the walking wounded.

My perfectionism was influential in that reversing of roles whereby I sought to receive counseling from my counselees. Because of the influence of the myth of perfection, I could not acknowledge my own needs for care. My needs went underground, but they surfaced in my attempts to care for others.

Sometimes as walking wounded we find ourselves in conflict with parishioners, with very little control over the conflict. James was such a person. There was a particular man in the church who continually challenged James's decisions and ideas. He was greatly frustrated. He spent many sleepless nights thinking about it.

James is African American. He grew up in a culture where peers made fun of others' physical stature; since childhood, he had been teased because he was short. He was a victim of what is called "sounding" or "woofing," in which someone protects his or her own identity by ridiculing another (Oliver, 1994). Usually, anyone who takes the brunt of constant woofing finds his or her identity devastated. So when James was called to ministry, he began to receive a level of respect that he had never known. He promised himself that he would never again be disrespected. But his feelings from childhood were close to the emotional surface. Thus, when the parishioner in James's church challenged him, he felt disrespected and deeply angry. He became so preoccupied with dealing with this man that the conflict eventually led to James's losing the church.

The walking wounded have a certain personal style that prevents receiving nurture and care. Zelda's mother was very young when Zelda was born, and she felt she could not raise her daughter. Consequently, Zelda grew up as an only child, in a home with her aging Jamaican grandparents. She was a very obedient, very responsible child. Zelda made a lot of the decisions and seemed to become an adult before her time. People came to her for advice even while she was a child. She received a lot of rewards for being adultlike and taking responsibility for her grandparents. The culture in which she grew up emphasized the traditional African value of care for aging elders (Wimberly, 1997).

Zelda accepted her call to ministry in her mid-forties and started her own independent church. She found herself playing the role of minister similarly to the role she had played as a child. She was very responsible, and people brought their problems to her. However, she grew resentful and found she did not have the energy needed to continually care for others. She felt she was giving generously but receiving very little. She began to avoid her parishioners and not answer her calls. Eventually, she was hospitalized for complete exhaustion. Medical personnel advised her to learn how to take better care of herself. She, too, was one of the walking wounded in need of care.

Something keeps us walking wounded from working on our own needs. Sometimes it is related to images of perfection. At other times, we lack recognition of our own need for care and nurture. We don't feel we have permission to take time to care for our own needs. So we never learn to transform our own woundedness into a resource to be used in caring. As walking wounded and wounded healers, we need times of retreat and care to tend to our own needs so that we can return to the caring task of providing good enough empathy.

A Theological Base for Wounded Healers

A detrimental aspect of the myth of perfection is that it blinds us to the meaning of the call to ministry. The biblical and theological roots of the call go back to the prophetic tradition of Israel, yet they influence our understanding of the call today. This prophetic image of the call is not rooted in perfection. It is based on God's transformation of the ordinary person into a servant of God. Thus, the origin of ministry is in God—not in the caregiver.

The call of Isaiah illustrates what the call means for the wounded healer. In Isaiah 6:1–13, the prophet's call includes his announcing his woundedness and vulnerability, to which an angel of the Lord attends. The prophet declares of himself: "And I said: 'Woe is me! For I am lost: for I am a man of unclean lips, and I dwell in the midst of a people of unclean lips; for my eyes have seen the King, the Lord of hosts!'" (Isaiah 6:5)

The same is true in Jeremiah 1:4–9, where Jeremiah felt unfit to be a prophet because as a youth with little experience he felt vulnerable. In verse 6, he says: "Ah, Lord God! Behold, I do not know how to speak, for I am only a youth." The prophet Moses was also viewed as wounded and vulnerable in the Book of Exodus. In being called, Moses found that God gave him words to equip him for the task.

In Isaiah chapters 41 to 43, we have a fuller picture of the call and its implications for carrying out ministry. God promises companionship to these servants as they execute God's call (41:10). God promises to uphold them, strengthen them, and enable them in their work; God promises to give them God's spirit so that they can carry out their given tasks (43:1). Moreover, God is portrayed as redeeming those who are called from their past sins and vulnerabilities.

Jesus' understanding of his own call is also grounded in the prophetic tradition of the Old Testament. While the Gospel writers do not portray him as having to be cleansed, he is baptized and otherwise seen as a human being (this is evident in his experience in the wilderness) and in need of empowerment by God's Spirit following baptism.

The call tradition that I have emphasized so far is male-oriented. This does not mean that women are excluded from God's call. I do indeed envision women as being under the same prophetic tradition of the call as men. Narrative understandings of Scripture and women's participation in interpreting Scripture have allowed us to discern women's inclusive participation as disciples in the ministry of God. For example, Elisabeth Schussler Fiorenza's *In Memory of Her: A Feminist Reconstruction of Christian Origins* helps us place women's stories in the stories of Jesus; she discovers also that women were called disciples and had roles equal to those of men. She concludes (and I concur) that "Only when we place the Jesus stories about women into the overall story of Jesus and his movement in Palestine are we able to recognize their subversive character. In the discipleship of equals the 'role' of women is not peripheral or trivial, but at the center, and thus of utmost importance to the praxis of 'solidarity from below'" (Fiorenza, 1992, p. 152).

Analysis of the call centrally emphasizes God's call of those who were not perfect, but inadequate. Fiorenza also emphasizes that women were included in the call as themselves being ordinary and imperfect: "The Jesus movement articulates a quite different understanding of God because it had experienced in the praxis of Jesus a God who called not Israel's righteous and pious but its religiously deficient and its social underdogs. In the ministry of Jesus God is experienced as all-inclusive love, letting the sun shine and the rain fall equally on the righteous and on sinners" (p. 130).

To spell out the import of these examples from the Old and New Testament prophets, first of all salvation is something that God does. Human beings are called by God to assist in this process. Second, God equips those called and makes them ready by whatever means are necessary. Third, God becomes a companion to the called; they are not in it by themselves. Fourth, perfection is not a requirement for the call. Finally, the lead and the energy for executing the call come from God.

The problem with the myth of perfection is that it contradicts the understanding of the call that is found in the prophetic tradition. The perfectionistic myth is anchored in a form of "works righteousness" that puts the focus on the minister's effort and leaves God out. Moreover, the perfectionist myth joins with another myth, "narcissistic individualism," that denies God's companionship along the way in ministry (Messer, 1989, p. 81). In addition, the perfectionistic myth forces its adherents to buy into the myth of "triumphalism," which denies the reality of suffering and vulnerability. In all these ways, the perfectionistic myth denies the need for God and God's involvement in our ministries.

As the walking wounded, we make biblical and theological understanding of the call to ministry secondary. We deny our need to be redeemed. We seek the power for ministry from within ourselves. We see no need, or deny the need, for God to be our companion.

Given both the pervasive influence of the perfectionistic myth and our tendency to deny our woundedness, spiritual renewal is essential. The approach of this book is to reconnect us with our call and examine it in light of whether or not we are wounded healers, the walking wounded. We also try to clarify the things in our lives that prevent our call from transforming us into wounded healers. The key idea is to be aware first that we must update our call regularly, and second that it requires spiritual retreat and renewal.

A Model for Reauthoring Mythologies

Our task is to reedit, or reauthor, our own mythologies where they make it difficult to carry out our call. In reauthoring the myths in our lives, we assume that the call from God is ongoing. God's call is like an unfolding drama in which new meaning is disclosed daily, and as the called we are invited to participate in these new meanings and possibilities.

Several related theoretical concepts give shape to how this unfolding of the call influences the lives of those called. One important concept is liminality. The term *liminality* suggests a threshold of perception. I use it to describe a period of retreat wherein we must suspend the ordinary routine of life so as to have time to regroup. The intention in such a liminal period is to allow the call to resurface. It is an "in-between" time when new models of reality are disclosed (Doehring, 1995, p. 143). Amid the suspension of routine, the call is an action story, a "deep narrative of the soul," where God's intentions for our lives can be made clear, to give focus and shape to our experiences (p. 142). The call is a shaping story that creates new meanings so that our lives and ministry regain freshness and are renewed. During the liminal period, the call crosses a threshold of perception and brings new meaning, a new world, a new self, and a new future.

The walking wounded who are called confront a problem: the moments of liminality are easily obscured, and new possibilities and breakthroughs are easily frustrated. Spiritual renewal helps attend to what is blocking our awareness so that it is no longer an obstacle to renewed meaning in life.

The process of editing the various myths so as to foster liminality follows several steps and poses important questions as we proceed. First, we identify the themes that inform our lives; can we see effects of the personal, marital, family, and ministerial myths? Step two is to assess whether these themes or the related myths are producing growth in ourselves and others; or are they contributing to our remaining wounded? Step three discerns the ongoing, continuously unfolding nature of our call; what is it doing to bring renewal to the life themes and myths at work in our lives? Finally, step four sets goals; can we make plans to alter our myths and bring them in line with our continuing call?

2

PERSONAL MYTHS

STORIES THAT EMPOWER US
OR LEAVE US VULNERABLE

RELIGIOUS CAREGIVING can be hazardous to your health. It is important for all religious caregivers to hear what the authors of *The Psychology of Clergy* say about the hazards inherent in the ministry:

> Ministry is just as much a hazardous occupation as that of high-rise window washing or stunt car driving. In fact, all of the "helping professions" are hazardous in the sense that they include a high danger of burnout and a high risk of fallout. Burnout can be seen in those who become fatigued, discouraged, and overwhelmed. Fallout can be seen in those who leave one vocation and enter another. While it is not likely that clergy will plunge ten stories to their deaths, as those perched near the top of skyscrapers might, still, they are constantly exposed to dangers that could threaten their mental health, their judgment, and their motivation [Malony and Hunt, 1991, p. 33].

We do, indeed, face hazards in ministry and caregiving. We face temptations, whether to be sexually indiscreet or to misuse our role and power to fulfill some personal need at the expense of others' needs. We face role conflicts, when as willing caregivers we spend more time in the roles that are demanded of us than in the ones we would prefer. And we face our own unresolved family-of-origin issues, as they are aggravated by the expectations of those who receive our care.

Then there is the inability to allow ourselves to be human and in need of care; the dysfunctional myths we cling to in our personal, marital, family, and ministerial lives; and denial of our need for the support of others. Regardless of the specific problem that arises, our personal beliefs and convictions—about ourselves, about our relationships with others, and about our world—play a crucial part in how we manage the hazards of religious caregiving.

Clarity about four kinds of myth—personal, marital, family, and ministerial—is essential. We need to understand the myths so as to "reauthor" them. Failure to find clarity and to reauthor the myths leaves us completely vulnerable to the hazards and the stresses related to them. We must identify and assess the myths before we can decide to alter our responses; only then can we facilitate our personal and professional growth as caregivers.

This chapter presents common myths from these four areas of our lives and work. Because they are so common, we must lift them up for scrutiny. They suffuse our ingrained convictions and beliefs about ourselves, others, and the ministry. Such deep convictions and beliefs are intrinsic to the fact of hazard in our profession.

Origins of Personal Myths

A personal mythology is made up of the convictions and beliefs that we hold about ourselves. It is made up of specific themes (Bagarozzi and Anderson, 1989), including:

Early memories

Whether or not we feel welcomed and wanted

Our birth order in relationship to other siblings

Gender

Name and nickname

Peer and sibling relationships

Roles we played (or still play) in our family of origin

Parental discipline in our family of origin and in school

How our parents relate(d) to each other

The stories with which we identify

As we see from the list, these themes have their genesis in our family of origin and our early childhood experiences. They are symbolic in nature and laden with affect (which is defined as "the conscious subjective aspect of an emotion considered apart from bodily changes"). The themes have several components, notably the internalized and externalized relationships that we have with significant others early in our lives and how the self interprets experience. They form a basic narrative, an overarching frame of reference that governs our feelings about ourselves, our relationships with others, and how we behave in the world. Lifelong interpretations and narratives become permanent parts of our self; we act to perpetuate them, which is why we confront change reluctantly. They assist us in developing a lifestyle or a pattern of existence that affects every situation we face. This thematic narrative is formative, and once formed it is difficult to change.

Personal myths have their roots in the way we cognitively organize our thinking as we interpret reality. They also have theoretical roots: in object relations theory, self-psychology, and family systems theories (Bagarozzi and Anderson, 1989; Gabbard, 1994).

The first two of these theories offer a perspective from depth psychology. Object relations theory focuses on how we as individuals internalized the positives and negatives we saw in significant others, and how we then go on to form a structure of the self that interprets reality from this basis. Self-psychology focuses on how we as individuals respond empathically to our externalized relationships with significant others, and how the responses impact our sense of self positively or negatively.

Family systems theory deals with how the interactions of marital and family members influence the growth of others. Later chapters say more specifically about family systems theories; this chapter largely stays in the depth psychological dimensions of the personal myth.

As we easily suspect, perfectionism is an important factor in how the themes of our narrative play out. The empathic responses of our significant others have great impact on how we interpret reality and form our personal myths. For instance, according to self-psychology theory, if significant others fail to show us empathy early in childhood, we will interpret ourselves as being worthless and without regard. Such an interpretation might lead us to seek to be perfect, or perform perfectly, to gain from the significant other the regard that we hunger for (Gabbard, 1994).

Personal myths are significant because they form the basis of all our interactions and experience with others. They improve or lessen the quality of our interactions and our ability to interpret our experience. If our personal myths are healthy and we feel positive about ourselves, then our interactions and experiences with others are enhanced. The reverse is also true. Those of us who believe we are called and who have good self-esteem generally treat hostility received from others as part of the job, and we do not take criticism personally. Those of us who have negative convictions about ourselves often take criticism as an attack upon ourselves, and we experience a deflation of our self-esteem. Good personal myths help us deal positively with the potential for self-sabotage; negative myths make us more vulnerable.

Common Personal Myths

I have encountered certain personal myths in retreats, in classes, and in my counseling with others. My selection of certain myths here is not exhaustive; there are many possible types. In fact, your own mythologies may be quite different. Yours may incorporate elements and themes of some of these myths but not of others. I intend only to spark your thinking about your own mythology by giving you a range of vivid examples I have observed with religious caregivers. I use the same rationale for presenting the other three types of myths—marital, family, and ministerial—in Chapters Three and Four.

THE MYTH OF REJECTION. A common myth that I have noted among religious caregivers is the myth of rejection. In any workshop or class, at least one or two people are convinced that they are rejected and unwanted by their significant others.

The myth of rejection is the belief that you are unwanted, even unwelcome, in life. It often stems from childhood experiences in the family of origin; sometimes it originates in the "womb or birth mythologies." These are stories told to us by significant others about our conception, the time in the womb, our birth, and the first six to twelve months of our existence (Rizzuto, 1979). The stories are significant because we read into them clues as to how we were welcomed to the world. They also give us our earliest sense of who God is. How we are welcomed into the world initially lays the groundwork for our experience of graceful acceptance from God as we grow up.

The myth of rejection makes us highly vulnerable to the myth of perfection. When we feel unwanted and unacceptable, we respond by trying to win love and affection from others. If those who withhold the possibility of being loved have high expectations around our performance in life, then we who feel rejected may go on to try to meet these demanding expectations.

Fran is a middle-age white woman who came to a spiritual retreat for chaplains. She discussed what she had found out about the circumstances surrounding her birth. Because she was adopted, she had a great need to put together a phantom genealogy, a make-believe heritage of her own.

The need came from a deep feeling that she was wanted by neither her biological nor her adoptive family.

She worked hard to find out about her biological parents. A cooperative social worker at an adoption agency found a letter from her birth mother that filled in some of the reasons she had been given up for adoption. The letter showed that Fran was actually wanted by her biological mother, but the circumstances of her conception and birth were very difficult. At the time, her mother was nineteen and Catholic; because her father was Protestant, Fran's mother's parents had the marriage annulled for religious reasons and forced her birth mother to put Fran up for adoption.

A genogram is a written- or drawn-out structure of three or more generations of a family. Fran developed a phantom genogram, based on her adopted family and what she could find out about her biological family. Piecing together more information from the adoption records and from answers to questions she asked her adoptive parents, Fran filled in the gaps of her early life. Where there was no information, she supplied it with her imagination. Motivating it all was a gnawing sense of not being wanted. (Often in such cases of feared rejection, the person has to search for the truth before any inner peace will come.)

Fran's feeling of not being wanted was dually based. She knew she had been adopted, but she felt she really did not fit with her adoptive family either. The feeling grew that something was missing in her life; it was deepened by the discovery that she had actually been welcomed into the world by her biological mother. Believing that her real name was Hilda (as she discovered when she obtained her adoption records) permitted her to imagine that Hilda was mature, self-assured, and self-assertive, just the opposite of Fran.

Fran's need to fill in the gaps and give herself a phantom history is the need of all human beings to sense a reason for being born. This in turn is basic to our experience of who we are in life, and feelings that we are not wanted powerfully influence how we feel about ourselves and our significance in this world. Fran's myth of rejection made her vulnerable to a variety of hazards in the ministry. She desired to belong, to be part of a family. If left unattended to or unmet, her desire could cause her call to caregiving to become instead a search for a family. She might inappropriately turn the concerns of her ministry primarily to herself and her own needs, rather than to those who are entrusted to her care.

THE MYTH OF POWERLESSNESS. Another myth I often encounter among caregivers is powerlessness. This myth is not as obvious since we often hide our feelings of powerlessness, from ourselves and others. Facing a difficulty or crisis could make us quite aware of being powerless.

The myth of powerlessness is the conviction that we have no real power or agency to impact our lives and the lives of others, our environment, and our world. We see other people as having more power and control over our lives than we do. We feel that things happen to us, that we have no real choice or decision. We may feel victimized by others, helpless to respond to what is being done "to us." We may become overly vigilant, seeking to identify potential perpetrators before they can abuse us.

The danger of perfectionism is that we might see ourselves unrealistically as imperfect or flawed. In our expectations of perfection, there is no possibility for grace-filled self-acceptance. The others whom we envisage as perfect have all the power.

In ministering, it is essential to claim power (Glover-Wetherington, 1996). We learn to feel confident in our ministerial identity, functioning and affirming our gifts for ministry. "Affirming our power" does not mean power over anyone or the power to dominate; it means being empowered to do what God has called us to do. If we are to be effective in ministry, we need to learn to claim the power that we have.

A sense of powerlessness hinders our ability to be in ministry. Feelings of powerlessness come mainly from our experiences in our family of origin. There are also racial and gender factors that make it difficult for women and African Americans to claim their power.

Miriam Anne Glover-Wetherington, a professor at Duke University Divinity School, points out how difficult it is for women to claim their power. She writes that women are socialized to act vulnerable, passive, tender, gentle, supportive, and powerless; they hide their strength because to display it is taken as being unfeminine. The result is that women's strengths, abilities, perceptions, and opinions are often not affirmed (Glover-Wetherington, 1996).

Historically, African Americans have also been prevented from claiming power in the wider culture. This sense of powerlessness in the majority culture is often accompanied by resort to negative power within the African American community. The sexism among African American men toward African American women is often an attempt to affirm the power that is denied in the larger culture. Violence against other African Americans is also a compensatory, but distorted, understanding of power (Oliver, 1994).

It is my experience that cultural images of what it means to be powerful and powerless are mediated through family relationships; thus, family-of-origin issues cannot be neglected. Minner, who is white and in his late twenties, has what he calls his "dining room table memory":

This memory involves a rectangular table, with me at about age six sitting at the end of the table (at the position many people might say the head of the table sits) with my parents on each side of me. And as I remember the scene, my parents turn to me and ask me which one of them I love the most. Having asked my parents about the memory, and them having no recollection of the scene, I have come to realize that whether the episode actually happened or not matters little. What matters is that memory represents some very valid feelings I have had growing up in my family of origin. I have felt many times as if I were trapped between my mom and dad. And this theme has run throughout my life. It has manifest[ed] itself in trying to take responsibility for others, trying to please others, and feeling a deep sense of guilt and shame when I try to claim my own power or boundaries. I feel like my parents abused me and took advantage of me unfairly.

This early childhood memory definitely gives a clue to the reality behind the helplessness that Minner feels today. He was trapped, not old enough to have any impact on what he felt his parents were doing to him. Feelings of powerlessness begin with being abused by significant others in life; there are real bases for feeling victimized and trapped (Poling, 1996).

While the basis of the myth of powerlessness is real, we who were victimized are responsible for *how* we remember the early experiences and *how* we form beliefs about ourselves and others (May, 1972). We may have been victimized, but we do not have to form a victim mythology or a myth of powerlessness. We are responsible for forming a myth, with its beliefs about our own impotence and ineffectiveness—as well as our own inability to confront what power we actually have.

A mythology of victimization or powerlessness can have a very negative impact on our caregiving. If we view those who seek our care as similar in any way to the abusers, it will be very difficult to respond positively to their legitimate needs. We might distance or disengage from the careseeker, to prevent being victimized again. We might rationalize the distancing by telling ourselves consciously that we don't want to be walked on again like a doormat.

We who feel powerless cannot ignore the fear of being victimized again. Yet the victim mythology may prevent us from responding to someone's genuine needs, for fear of disengaging or becoming combative with a parishioner or careseeker. We need to edit our victim mythology so that we can distinguish potentially real victimization from our own projection of victimization, that is, projection when there is no substantial threat of being victimized.

Minner has explored the themes at work in his myth of powerlessness in the hope of being able to distinguish real victimization from projected victimization. Exploring early memories and mapping their influence on his life helped him to identify the themes. As a religious caregiver himself, Minner faces the hazard of "finding" perpetrators of abuse where there are none. Clearly, the impact on his ministry is potentially devastating. We can also see the importance of not ignoring or excusing real abuse at the hands of parishioners or those for whom we care. When real abuse occurs, an appropriate response is very important for our spiritual and mental health. Recognition of our myth of powerlessness and victimization is the first step in learning to distinguish between real victimization and projected victimization.

THE MYTH OF THE LONER. Some ministers prefer to go it alone in ministry, for any of a variety of reasons. Some of these become apparent as I explore the meaning of the myth of the loner.

A person who perceives himself or herself to be a loner distrusts the world. The loner fears getting emotionally close, fears being hurt or disappointed. He or she desires closeness, but intimacy is threatening. The loner believes he or she is alone in the world; indeed, this person prefers working alone and prizes and protects privacy.

This fear of closeness is accompanied by a belief that we are unrealistically flawed and imperfect. Isolation from close relationships helps us handle the overwhelming sense of imperfection. But wishing to be perfect is still deeply rooted in our sense of self, and so we loners are often preoccupied with perfection, especially when relationships hamper our efforts.

My own birth mythology reveals a loner mythology. I never knew my birth mythology until my mother told my wife, and my wife told me. After I learned it from my wife, both my father and my mother talked about it as well.

My parents were married in 1939. They believed that it was important not to let marriage and children interfere with achieving individual goals for education and professional development. Consequently, they waited two years after being married to consider having children. But they were rushed into it before they were ready.

According to the story they tell, my dad was pastoring a church some eighty miles from where they lived. He also worked during the week for the government in a factory that made cloth goods for the military. Because World War II was beginning, Dad was expected to give priority to his job; he was expected to work even on the weekends. He told his supervisor that he could not work on Sunday because he was pastoring a church and had duties there. His supervisor said, "Either work or fight."

He realized the consequences, but my dad went to church that Sunday, and the following week he was told to report for military service. When the bishop realized what was happening, he acted to intervene with the selective service. In the meantime, my parents had decided to have children, thinking that if Dad had to go into the military he might be killed and there would be no children born to their union. My brother was born in November 1942, and I was born eleven months later, on October 22, 1943. The bishop's intervention succeeded, and Dad continued to pastor and work for the government.

The birth narrative continued, with my mother suffering from what is today called postpartum depression. She was exhausted from the first pregnancy, and becoming pregnant two months after the birth of her first child was too much. Shortly after I got home I had to be put back into the hospital so that my mother could get rest.

I speculate that my propensity for being a loner stems from this event. I often prefer to be alone—and I also detest being in the way. I will do anything not to be a burden to anyone. These themes in my birth mythology help me identify the themes that operate in my life today. For example, I have a hard time relaxing and not working. In December 1994 I had heart bypass surgery. Following this emergency, I have really looked at my own personal mythology and have gone back to participating in my own personal therapy as a result. My pastoral counselor says that my life was spared so that I could learn to love and be loved. I interpret this to mean that my theme of being a loner has caused some deficit in my being able to give love as well as to receive love. This deficit appears to have originated in my birth mythology. My coming to this world caused a problem for my mother, and my life has been spent trying not to be a problem for others—not to be close to others.

The danger of the loner mythology for the ministry is our being disengaged and isolated from the people for whom we have caring responsibility. We often view them as intruders into our time and as threats to our privacy. This can lead parishioners to feel neglected and uncared for. My own style of relating to people is either to pastor small churches or to have counseling appointments. I have difficulty seeing people who just stop by without appointments; I vigorously protect my free time from what I feel are intrusions. This is how I accommodate my awareness of my personal mythology. The older I get, the more I am able to allow other people close to me. However, there is much room for improvement.

THE MYTH OF THE GOOD GIRL. Many women who pursue the ministry bring with them a conventional understanding of what it means to be "nice girls." Although ministry is a nontraditional undertaking for women, stereotypical images of femininity are always lurking in the background. Even the feminist and "womanist" impulses of many women do not keep traditional images of what it means to be female from emerging. And early expectations in the home can have a lasting impact, as an African American pastor in her late twenties reveals:

> I was always told to be a "good girl," and it seems I was determined to do just that. My mother referred to being a good girl as respecting authority, listening, and doing what I was told. I was always told to pay attention to those in authority and listen to my elders. Good girls are rewarded, I was told.

The myth of the good girl is the conviction that you must be good and gracious at all costs. It is rooted in feelings that you cannot be angry or upset because this will make others uncomfortable. The goal is perfect goodness.

The pastor quoted above learned to suppress her feelings about her abuse at the hands of authority figures. This also concealed an entire aspect of her personality and silenced an important part of who she was. To be an effective minister, she had to rediscover what was silent and give it voice. It was essential to recover her anger toward abusive authority figures in order to develop responses to authority that went beyond "good girl."

Working to reclaim her voice was hard. As long as she tried to meet the good-girl expectations, she remained depressed and could not provide appropriate care for her parishioners. The good girl was always silent, when she needed to speak up.

This person suffered from what Beth Erickson calls the "goodness code" (Erickson, 1993). She points out that, from many centuries of socialization, this code of overresponsibility makes the care of relationships primarily an assignment given to women. Women are the relational experts; they have the capacity for sensitive, intuitive, generous, nurturing, and genuine comforting. Sometimes this capacity is overdone and leads to self-sacrifice and burnout. The goodness code can lead women caregivers to take full responsibility for the success of relationships at all costs, for overconcern about the approval of others, and for the very lives of others. This theme of goodness at all costs needs editing if the person is to gain any effectiveness in ministry.

The goodness code crosses racial lines. African American girls and women feel the same pressures to be good girls; they, too, make decisions about being silent or speaking up. However, evidence suggests that the socialization of African American girls is less stereotypical than for white middle- and upper-class girls (Taylor, Gilligan, and Sullivan, 1995). While African American girls are raised to assume traditional female roles of nurturing and child care, evidence also suggests they are encouraged to be self-sufficient, to stand up for themselves, and to fight back. However, my experience with clients and others is that in the case of abuse, especially sexual abuse, silence is the norm.

THE MYTH OF INVULNERABILITY. The myth of invulnerability is a major theme in the lives of most ministers. I have found it the most prevalent myth in my teaching in seminary. Even in retreats, ministers seem to need permission from the leader and others to be open about their vulnerability. In a competitive and success-oriented culture being vulnerable is a liability. Not recognizing our vulnerability and using it appropriately is a liability as well.

Many students come to talk to me about clinical pastoral education. Some call it "ministry through navel gazing." These are people who have difficulty letting others see their mistakes and hang-ups, that is, being vulnerable.

Some of us were taught that vulnerability and weakness—signs of human imperfection—are disastrous and must be avoided at all costs. We who have learned stereotypical male and female roles characteristically find it hard to deal with our vulnerable side, by which I mean we are told that just having certain feelings (fear, tenderness, warmth, anxiety, and others) is a sign of weakness. For us men, these are inappropriate, unmasculine feelings that should be avoided; for women, these feelings are risky and could lead to harm (Taylor, Gilligan, and Sullivan, 1995). To deny feelings of vulnerability is to embrace the myth of invulnerability.

Being in touch with our feelings of vulnerability is essential for the caring ministry. They help us empathize with others. Denying the feelings takes away some of our humanness and makes it difficult to connect, care for, and be intimate with others. The effective caregiver in ministry moves beyond the stereotypical images of what it means to be male and female, so we can be more human and more responsive to the needs of others.

It is important to realize the gender issues related to being vulnerable. Because women are taught to be vulnerable (Glover-Wetherington, 1996), it is important to recognize that claiming vulnerability for women has its limitations. Women need to balance affirming their strengths with recognizing their limitations and vulnerabilities (Snorton, 1996). A "code of masculinity" also deserves attention. The code prescribes that men must dread, abhor, and deny feeling vulnerable, weak, or helpless (Erickson,

1993). Consequently, we male caregivers are often out of touch with our feelings; we find it hard to be aware of them. Even though our family-of-origin experiences have prepared us well to be caregivers, we often seek to be carers in characteristic ways that prevent us from getting too close emotionally. We often maintain emotional distance from those for whom we care. The more we men caregivers are in touch with our nurturing and tender sides, the more effective we can be. We may prefer to be problem solvers because we have difficulty being emotionally present or available to those with problems who need our care.

THE MYTH OF SOLE RESPONSIBILITY. Ministers of both genders may suffer from an overblown sense of responsibility. The myth of sole responsibility relates to the conviction that what happens in life depends solely on us. It is a heavy burden, accompanied by the feeling that because no one else can carry the responsibility we are left all alone to do so. We often feel drained and tired; burnout is always a prospect. The feeling comes from early childhood, from prematurely taking on adult responsibilities, hence from trying to be perfect in meeting unrealistic expectations. We often recognize a loss of childhood, and a feeling that one is doomed to a life of being burdened. Having tried to be perfect in meeting the expectations of premature adult responsibility as a child, we find that a sense of unconscious futility persists into adulthood.

Self-abuse is a hazard of the myth of sole responsibility. Some of us had parents who were substance abusers. Or our parents reversed roles with us children. Both of Edna's parents were alcoholics and ineffectual as parents. Edna is white, the oldest child; she was assigned the role of caring for her younger brothers and sisters. In her ministry, she entered fully into caring for others, but she often felt resentful about it. It got to the point where she could not hide her resentment, and she had difficulty functioning. While the resentment was strong, she could not release herself from the role, because she believed that she was the only person who could make a difference in the lives of others. She felt that only she could solve the problems of others.

THE MYTH OF SELF-SACRIFICE OR UNLOVABILITY. This myth is not as common as the preceding myths. Yet occasionally I run across people in ministry who sacrifice themselves because they feel unloved and hope to gain the love of others.

This myth relates to the belief that we will only be loved if we hide our true selves. The love we received as children was often conditional, based on performing up to others' expectations, to the detriment of self. A major theme in this myth is unrequited or unreturned love. We hide our real selves, burying deeply our anger about having to sacrifice selfhood. One woman pastor of my acquaintance said she feared that if she allowed her real self to be known, people would not like her. Therefore, she hid her self and tried to keep certain aspects of her personality under wraps.

Self-sacrifice has a gender component. Pointing out that women are socialized to sacrifice themselves, Brita Gill-Austern (1996) draws some important conclusions. First, women are raised to consider and take care of the needs of others, especially men and children. Second, women must sacrifice themselves and their needs in order to remain connected and maintain relationships. Third, structural inequities exist in society, and economic and social dependence reinforce self-sacrifice. And fourth, self-abnegation, self-doubt, and false guilt often motivate self-sacrifice; such a view of love prevents women from claiming the voice that they have.

Gill-Austern identifies the devastating influences of women's self-sacrifice: loss of a sense of self and of voice, loss of connection with their own needs and desires, feelings of anger and resentment for being victimized, over-functioning with regard to others, underfunctioning on behalf of self, undermining their capacity for genuine mutuality and intimacy, and abdication of using publicly all of their God-given gifts.

Parishioners and those for whom we care may feel grateful for having persons around who are invariably pleasant. Yet how many of us are dying inside, because we don't dare let our true selves be known? We are intimidated by feeling that we could not possibly be loved for ourselves.

THE MYTH OF THE SAVIOR. Given our childhood and family-of-origin experiences, the myth of the savior is one to which many ministers are prone. We are prime candidates for developing this myth because of the sometimes limitless hopes that others bring to us.

The myth of the savior is the conviction that our role in life remains to bring stability and peace to the "family." This role can be negative or positive, depending on whether we have received the nurturing and support we need in order to grow. More precisely, a family can provide an emotional atmosphere where we are each encouraged to grow into a unique person. A family environment in which we are sidetracked, if we want to be accepted, into taking on a designated family role or expectations that stifle growth is debilitating to our personal growth.

Michael was the oldest son of a family living in the Caribbean. He was born after his mother had a series of miscarriages. Because her pregnancy with him went smoothly, his parents felt he was special. Therefore, while he was a child they dedicated him to God, feeling that God had brought him into the world for a special reason. When his parents told him the circumstances of his birth, he too accepted his specialness and sought to fulfill their expectations through ministry. Family members responded to him as if he were a savior to them.

George was also special to his family. However, he was born while his parents were having tremendous marital conflict. His mother had had an affair several years before her pregnancy and kept it hidden from her husband. George's father found out and was going to leave his wife, when she told him she was pregnant. He suspended his plans to leave when the pregnancy proved difficult. Following George's birth, his father stayed on. His mother felt that George had saved the marriage.

George's mother told him this story often; she relied on him for many things. He felt she was constantly expecting him to perform the role of savior of the family; he had no life of his own. Others in George's life, too, saw him as someone who could rescue them from pain and suffering. Although he was intimidated by these expectations, he felt very bad when he could not deliver people from their pain. Anxiety about not being what others wanted him to be led to health problems. He was often very sick, and parishioners were upset when he was not available to them. But by being sick, he found the only way he could relax.

THE MYTH OF ALOOFNESS. The loner is convinced of his or her ineptness in close relationships. In the myth of aloofness, we believe that emotional closeness is dangerous. We must stay disengaged or disconnected from relationships in order to be a self. As aloof persons, we fear being swallowed up in relationships. We are intimidated and overwhelmed by the perfectionistic expectations of others, so we must remain aloof in order to survive emotionally.

Most often, aloof persons experienced a blurring of the role boundaries between children and adults. There might have been a reversal of roles, with the children expected to become the parent for the younger children in the family (or for the parents). Another blurring of boundaries is when the parent relates to the child as a peer and confidant; the child is expected to be the emotional companion to the parent, and the child has no opportunities to develop other relationships with peers. Sometimes the child feels threatened, afraid of being taken over and smothered. The child learns to survive by distancing from others.

The myth of aloofness is not common among ministers, in my experience. I include it here as a myth that exists; with growing numbers of clergy addicted sexually and relying on fantasy to motivate them, it is important to include this myth here. Indeed, some people sexualize relationships or turn to fantasy as protection against intimacy or emotional closeness.

Melton was reared in a family where he became very close to his mother. She relied on him, especially when his father was emotionally unavailable. While their relationship never crossed any sexual boundaries, she was often partially undressed in his presence. Melton always felt that there was a sexual quality to their relationship that he found very threatening. He developed an interest in pornography early in adolescence, which was his way of distancing himself from his mother.

Later, Melton developed dating patterns that were a series of one-night stands. He also frequented adult bookstores. He often worried that he might get caught in his activities and disgraced in the eyes of his parishioners. He made many unexpected trips out of town to satisfy his sexual needs and interests. He made up intricate lies to maintain his secret lifestyle, all the while avoiding dealing with his fears of being too close that stemmed from an overly close relationship to his mother. As much as he desired to be in relationships with others, it was too awkward for him emotionally.

Summary

Personal myths are the focus in this chapter. They foster our convictions and beliefs about ourselves and the world; they inform everything we do. Personal myths invariably have their origin in early childhood experiences.

The myths presented here are drawn from the lives of people whom I have encountered over the years in caregivers' retreats, in counseling, and in the classroom. The myths narrate the struggles in persons I have known; they are ones to which caregivers are prone because of their personalities and background experience. The selection of myths here is representative, but not exhaustive. Other myths are the subjects of the next few chapters.

Each myth connects with the myth of perfection. To win favor or love, those of us who are convinced of our unacceptableness seek to please others perfectly. Or we may be convinced of our own personal flaws and are therefore intimidated by others' expectations.

The myth of perfection is the well from which most of us as religious caregivers draw in developing our personal and ministerial myths. Not only is perfectionism the result of attempts to win favor and love despite our unacceptableness; we are urged by cultural expectations to be perfect. As religious caregivers, our lives are grounded in the Puritan heritage, whose perfectionistic expectations are nonnegotiable. We are to be exemplary in every way; we are to be almost godlike. Such expectations make religious caregivers particularly susceptible to certain myths.

I suggest that to reauthor our myths as religious caregivers, we must look consciously for a connection to the myth of perfection. In doing this, we find a great measure of freedom to be ourselves, as well as to respond to the needs of our careseekers.

Exercises

You may now want to identify some of the personal myths that are at work in your own life. Below are some exercises designed to help you do just that. For example, the first exercise deals with your earliest memory. Often, exploring the earliest memory reveals some of the themes that are currently at work in your life. The other exercises are designed to help you identify some of the myths that are at work and how they impact your life today, positively as well as negatively. Your birth myth, for instance, may be one that is very positive, and those exercises are designed to help you to get in touch with how your birth myth is working in your life today.

I recommended that you not try to do these exercises totally alone. It is good to have others accompany you on the journey. This not only provides companionship, but it is a good source of feedback on what you might find. If you decide to go it alone, be sure to have someone you can call so as to talk about what you are discovering. Journeying alone may increase a sense of isolation and continue to promote negative myths.

Personal myths deal with different areas of our early life; the questionnaire focuses on those areas.

PERSONAL MYTHOLOGY QUESTIONNAIRE

EXERCISE I Earliest Memory

1. What is your earliest memory of your family of origin?
2. After thinking about it, write down a few things you remember.
3. What themes do you see that were operating then?
4. In what ways are the same themes present in your life today?
5. How do these themes contribute to or take away from your present way of doing ministry?
6. How do these themes relate to your ability to discern God's presence in your life and ministry?

EXERCISE II   Birth Mythology

1. What circumstances, beliefs, and values do you think played a part in your parents' decision to have you?

2. What were your parents' reactions to discovering that your mother was pregnant with you?

3. What were your parents' reactions on seeing you for the first time?

4. Write down a few of your discoveries in recalling this information.

5. How do you feel that your welcome into this world influences your way of doing ministry today?

6. How does your welcome into the world influence your discerning God's presence in your life and in the church?

EXERCISE III   Birth Order

1. Where were you born in the family birth order?

2. Specifically, were you the first, second, last, or only child?

3. What does this mean in terms of your self-understanding now?

4. Pick a concrete example to illustrate your self-understanding.

EXERCISE IV   Gender and Sex

1. How do you think your mother felt about your sex?

2. How do you think your father felt about your sex?

3. How have their feelings contributed to your ministry today?

4. How have their feelings contributed to your sense that God is present in your life and in your ministry?

EXERCISE V   Names and Nicknames

1. Who named you?

2. Why were you given the name you have?

3. What roles are implied in your name?

4. What is your nickname?

5. Why were you given that nickname?

6. What roles are implied by it?

7. How has your name contributed to your ministry?

8. How has your name helped you to see God at work in you or in your ministry?

9. How has your nickname contributed to your ministry?

10. How has your nickname helped you to see God at work in you or in your ministry?

EXERCISE VI Peer and Sibling Relationships

1. How would you characterize your relationship with siblings (brothers and sisters) and peers?

2. Pick an example of what you feel has been most characteristic of your sibling and peer relationships.

EXERCISE VII Roles

1. What roles were you expected to play in your family of origin?

2. What roles did you actually play?

3. What were the costs (in love and affection) involved in not playing the role you were expected to play?

4. What were the payoffs from playing the role?

5. How do the roles that you played in your family of origin influence you today?

6. How have these roles contributed to or detracted from your ministry?

7. How have these roles enabled you to discern God's presence in your ministry?

EXERCISE VIII Parental/School Discipline

1. Typically, how were you disciplined as a child at home and at school?

2. What impact do you feel this had on you?

3. Give a specific example of discipline in your home and in your school.

EXERCISE IX   Parents' Relationship

1. What role were you expected to play when your parents had marital conflict? Were you expected to mediate or take sides, or did your parents resolve their differences without drawing you into their conflict?

2. How do you think your parents' expectations toward you and their marital relationship influence your ministry today?

3. How do you think your parents' expectations toward you and their marital relationship influence your ability to discern God at work in your life and ministry?

EXERCISE X   Story Identification

1. What is your favorite fairy tale, book, short story, play, movie, TV show, et cetera? Select only one or two examples.

2. Who is your favorite character, and why?

3. What happens to your favorite character throughout the story?

4. What happens to the character at the end?

5. What character do you dislike the most, and why?

6. What happens to the disliked character throughout the story?

7. What happens to the disliked character at the end?

8. How does your identification with these stories relate to your present ministry?

9. How do these identifications enable you to discern God's presence in your life and ministry?

ASSESSMENT I

1. Given the above exercises and categories, what is the dominant theme that you see running through your life?

2. What are some of the lesser or subthemes running through your life?

3. What is the major conviction or belief that you have about your life and existence? For example, do you feel loved, worthwhile, accepted? Do you feel you have to prove yourself to somebody? What do you think you have to prove?

4. Trace the cross-generational legacy of these themes. Can you see these themes present in your parents' lives, your grandparents' lives, and your great-grandparents' lives?

5. Can you see these themes at work in your offspring? (Answer if applicable.)

ASSESSMENT II

1. Can you discern God at work seeking to transform the themes into growth opportunities?

2. What plans do you need to make to transform these themes into possibilities for growth?

3

MARITAL AND FAMILY MYTHS

STORIES THAT AFFECT OUR
RELATIONSHIPS WITH LOVED ONES

I HAVE ENCOUNTERED some common marital and family myths among the people in my retreats, counseling, and classes. Marital myths examine the nature of the ideal-mate and ideal-marriage expectations. Family myths explore ideal-child and ideal-family expectations. In this chapter, we discuss the etiology of these ideal expectations in the family of origin, and the various life-cycle tasks involved in developing ideal marital and family expectations. The common marital myths to be explored are

- The myth of jubilation
- The myth of settling
- The myth of the parental substitute
- The myth of repudiating family-of-origin pitfalls
- The myth of the knight in shining armor
- The myth of unlimited affection
- The ideal-marriage myth of positive communication
- The myth of limited possibility in midlife

The common family myths that we explore are

- The myth of premature adult responsibility
- The myth of fulfilling the family legacy
- The myth of dire consequences

○ The myth of the family mediator

○ The myth of the family scapegoat

Marital and family myths help shape how we relate to our mates, our children, our extended families, our friends, our parishioners, and to the careseekers who come to us. Positive marital and family myths have a nurturing impact on others and also sustain us in our daily lives. Negative marital and family myths hinder our ability to be nurturing and caring; they drain us of our energy and our motivation for caring.

Two crucial signs that negative myths are at work in our lives are loss of energy and burnout. The tasks we undertake do not feel just demanding; they are burdensome. We may also have feelings of disappointment about our mate or our children; marital dissatisfaction may be high. We might feel caught in conflict with parishioners and believe we have very little control over it. Ideal expectations—of ourselves as well as others— often underlie all these feelings. Exploring our ideal images of marriage and family can help us identify some of the particular myths that are at work in our own lives.

The marital and family myths that I explore are the most common ones in the literature. They illustrate the myths I have so often encountered in my professional experience. Surely there are more marital and family myths that are not covered here.

The marital and family myths that affect religious caregivers are similar to those of the general population; our myths differ more in *intensity* than in kind. Religious caregivers are especially under pressure to have model marriages and families; this is because of the influence of the myth of perfection. As a result, the marital and family lives of religious caregivers are under greater scrutiny by the public than are marriages in the general public.

The Nature of Marital and Family Myths

Marital myths are beliefs about ideals: the perfect mate, the ideal marriage, and self as the ideal mate. Likewise, family myths are made up of ideal children, ideal parents, and ideal families.

Every individual, as a potential spouse, has definite ideals that he or she brings to courtship, engagement, and marriage. The ideal images constitute what we perceive as necessary for an ideal marriage. When two people meet, their ideal images come into dialogue. The dominant stories that emerge are the marital mythology and family mythology. A marital mythology is a cognitive narrative structure, the meshing of the ideal-mate and ideal-marriage images of both spouses. It represents consensus on what two people believe about marriage, marital expectations, marital roles, and general marital behavior. The myth reflects two sets of perceptions of the "perfect" family or family life.

A family mythology is a cognitive narrative structure made up of the meshing of ideal-family and ideal-children images held by both mates. It represents beliefs about family life, expectations, roles, and behavior.

This is how one person explains the ideal-mate image he brought to marriage:

> I always wanted a mate who was beautiful, honest, religious, sincere, caring, ambitious, intelligent, adventurous, charming, warmhearted, and sociable. She must have the fine qualities of a homemaker and a good cook, and be able to be a good mother to our children. She must also be able to stick with me and love me through rough times as we share and grow together spiritually, socially, and economically. I want someone I can share my life with, someone who is there for me, and I would be there for her in return. I would like someone to encourage me in all of my endeavors, someone to love and who is able to return that love.

This is a very detailed image of the ideal mate. The speaker developed it from watching and interacting with his parents and others within his community. We all have cognitive representations of ideal spouses that result from our experiences with significant others of the opposite sex and from experiences with family models of male-female relationships and husband-wife relationships (Bagarozzi and Anderson, 1989).

These ideal cognitive representations have conscious and unconscious components to them. These components develop because of the expectations that we bring from our families of origin. Most of our conscious ideal-spouse images are grounded in the expectation of repeating the positive experiences that we each encountered in our family of origin (Guerin, Fay, Burden, and Kautto, 1987). We expect that the negative experiences will somehow be minimized and replaced by positive experiences. Unconscious ideal-image components relate to unresolved personal problems stemming from early childhood.

Each spouse also comes to the marriage with some expectations about the ideal son and/or daughter. These expectations also have conscious and unconscious components; they relate to the roles that each spouse will play as a parent. Like the ideal-mate image, the conscious ideal-child image becomes a standard to which the actual child is compared. The unconscious component of this ideal-child image consists of unresolved conflicts in the personal lives of the parents that are reactivated by the presence of offspring. They center around certain developmental tasks that remain uncompleted in the adult parents' lives (Bagarozzi and Anderson, 1989).

Ideal images of marital and family life are often rooted deeply in culture, reflecting traditional notions of what it means to be male and female. A traditional man, or so the classic notion goes, is one who works outside the home, seeks his own autonomy and self-interests, denies the importance of feelings and relationships, values the marketplace over family life, talks rather than listens, prefers conflict to behind-the-scenes negotiation, is self-confident without humility, makes decisions without thoughtful pondering, prefers aggression to persuasion, and struggles for power and achievement (Hunter, 1990).

Traditional notions shape stereotypical views of women as well. The woman must make her home her domain, care for the relational needs of men and children, be a mother and dependent on her husband, define herself as derivative of the men in her life, deny her autonomy and agency, hide her true feelings, be an expert in interpersonal relationships, carry major responsibility for the relationships in her life, deny anger, and always put the needs of others before her own (Hunter, 1990). The ideal images that we bring to marriage and family are often steeped in these traditional images of men and women; the images often conflict with the realities that we encounter in living out family and marital life and thus need to be modified.

Whether or not our stereotypical images of family and marital life are valid, our families need positive family myths in order to function. A healthy, functioning family myth is one that enables each family member to grow and develop his or her full possibilities as a human being. In such a family, no one's growth and development is sacrificed for the benefit of others.

The family often encounters circumstances that necessitate revising the ideal images. Positive family myths nurture narratives that sustain family members through the stress of life-cycle, marital, and family transitions (Klagsbrun, 1985). These positive myths are nurturing during troubling times for the marriage and family; they provide resources for facing reality. Negative family myths, on the other hand, cause family members to sacrifice the growth of one or more family members during life-cycle, marital, and family stress.

Negative myths develop as a result of the family's anxiety in confronting threats, whether internal or external to the family (Pillari, 1986).

The function of the family is to develop myths or beliefs that help it confront threats. Failure to develop positive family myths weakens the family's ability to respond to threats.

The Caregiver's "Three Families"

Religious caregivers must attend to marital and family myths because the quality of our marital and family life impacts the quality of the ministry we undertake. Edwin Friedman talks about the pastor being part of several families (Friedman, 1985). The pastor is a member of the family of origin (the family into which he or she is born), the family of creation (the family the pastor and her or his spouse create), and the family of the church. What happens in the marital and family life of the pastor has direct impact on all these families. Friedman says that the pastor's or religious caregiver's unresolved marital and family problems also impact the relationships of those families connected to the church. Consequently, it is very important for us as religious caregivers to explore the ideal images that inform what we do in our marital and family life.

The crucial concern for us as religious caregivers is how much we invest emotionally in the three families with which we are involved. At times, we may need to focus our emotional energy on one while the other two are neglected. This causes conflict in the other families. Optimally, we learn to appropriately balance our emotional investments so we can be emotionally available without shortchanging any of the families. Of course, the priority of our emotional investment has to be our family of creation.

Congregations are greatly affected by the quality of the emotional investment we caregivers make (Friedman, 1985). Each of the three families develops some feeling for the nature of our emotional investment. When the investment changes in any way, each family knows it. The emotional balance is disturbed as a result.

The Common Marital and Family Myths

The ideal images that I discuss below all have some relationship to our emotional investments. Our ideal expectations about mate, children, marriage, and family impact the level of emotional investment we make.

The Myth of Jubilation

This myth of expectation is commonly found among religious caregivers who were assigned adult responsibility as children and who lost their childhood as a result.

One ideal-mate image is the expectation that our spouse creates an environment of joy that compensates for the childhood we lost while growing up. This unconscious myth holds that the spouse will stimulate unlimited joy and happiness.

Blake, an African American in his mid-twenties, brought such an expectation to his courtship and engagement. In particular, his ideal-mate expectation was for someone intelligent, well-mannered, youthful, and jubilant.

Blake was the first-born child. He became the parental child, the one assigned the responsibility of caring for his younger brothers and sisters. He felt the full weight of responsibility for them. Both his parents worked to earn enough financially for the family to survive. Because he was the oldest, Blake felt he missed out on some of the privileges and fun that should have been part of his growing up and that were extended to his younger siblings. When his father dedicated him to God as a child, he was consciously aware of the religious significance of the role he was to play in his adult life. At the time, the expectations made it easier to give up his childhood since he was rewarded with parental praise for taking on his responsible role.

When I met Blake, he had not found his ideal mate. He had met several possible mates but had not confronted any of the challenges to his expectations of an ideal mate. Unconsciously, he was waiting to meet someone who could compensate for his loss of childhood. But the human unconscious is generally of two minds; unconsciously Blake was also seeking a mate who would preserve his childhood role of self-sacrifice. But that was completely unbeknownst; such awareness of his dual motivation awaited the later, editing phase of his work with his myth of the ideal mate.

Blake's expectation followed traditional lines. His ideal mate would fit the conventional female image, and she would take major responsibility for keeping their relationship happy and—of course—perfect.

As a religious caregiver who had not yet found his ideal mate, and who had not yet experienced reconciling his ideal-mate image with a real mate, Blake had a lot of emotional energy, and time, that could be invested in caregiving. He did not seem eager to find his ideal mate. Rather, he put most of his time into his ministry.

The Myth of Settling

An important theme in ideal-mate expectations is that of settling. In my experience, settling is more commonly found among women ministers. Its themes grow out of cultural expectations of women.

A thirty-year-old African American, Brenda was an assistant minister in charge of youth work in her church. She had been raised in a home without a male presence; her mother divorced while Brenda was a very small child. She saw her mother pursue a life pattern of refusing to get involved with men, except very superficially. This meant an occasional date, but her mother never went out with a man more than once. She appeared very timid around men and was critical of them; she was completely dedicated to parenting.

Brenda knew her father; he was very kind to her. But he was often late with child support. It was Brenda's role to call her father when the payments were late to ask what was going on. Brenda's mother assigned her the role, refusing to take the responsibility herself. Her mother knew that Brenda was the apple of her father's eye and he loved her, so her mother used this fact to the family's advantage. The strategy worked; her father always followed up her phone call with a check. Obviously, Brenda was caught in a marital triangle, drawn into her parents' conflict even when they were no longer married.

Brenda was a very intelligent little girl. She knew exactly why she was calling her father, although her mother never told her why. She recognized that she was being used by both of them. But she cooperated because she knew she would have contact with her father whenever a payment was late. She even wondered if her father was deliberately late in order to talk to her. This manipulative strategy made her feel wanted.

This pattern of contacting her father when child-support payments were late contributed greatly to her adult pattern of "settling." In settling, a person decides to take less when more is possible. With regard to the image of the ideal mate, settling dictates that it is sufficient to find a mate who allows one to retain a vestige of the role played in the family of origin. Thus one settles for no more than what one experienced in childhood. In the language of ideal-mate expectations, the myth of settling essentially says, "If I can't have my ideal or perfect mate, I'll settle for the next best thing."

Brenda knew almost immediately that the man she was dating was not the best person for her. In fact, most of the potential mates she encountered fell far short of her ideal image, and she knew she would eventually marry someone of that sort. She stayed in relationships that were frustrating because she believed she could not do any better. Brenda was quick to settle.

As we might expect, Brenda seemed to be attracted to men who offered the same behavioral pattern she had experienced with her father. They tended to be older, had money, and were emotionally unavailable except when she determined to charm them. This pattern operated unconsciously until she reached age thirty, when her younger sister married someone Brenda thought was less than ideal for her sister. Brenda suddenly saw the pattern in her own life. She broke off a relationship with a man she was dating and made up her mind that she was going to change the pattern of settling too soon. A new desire emerged, for a man who was more emotionally available and more compatible with her educational and spiritual interests. Brenda put her efforts into her ministry, while waiting for a more realistic "Mr. Right." He would not be flawless, but his limitations would not prevent him from being emotionally present to her.

Brenda's role in her family of origin kept to traditional gender lines. It was her role to take on major responsibility for relationships with men. Settling, then, is a natural outgrowth of the cultural expectation that women are responsible for maintaining relationships.

Brenda's settling had an impact on her ministry. While she was in her settling pattern regarding a less-than-ideal mate, people in the church were aware that she was investing her emotional energy elsewhere. Those who worked closely with her began to ask what was wrong and why she was so preoccupied. They were aware that her emotional presence with them had changed.

The Myth of the Parental Substitute

It is common among people who join the ministry to have been prematurely assigned adult responsibility as children. In adulthood, they find that one typical way of carrying on adult responsibility is to care for "children." The myth of the parental substitute is the conviction that we have to be responsible for the lives of others—especially our parents. The roles we play belong to the previous generation, in which our parents failed to provide for their own needs.

Wolfgang began to explore his ideal-mate image at a retreat. He was white, thirty years old, the son of a European immigrant to the United States. His ideal of a mate was someone who would meet the needs that his parents did not meet for him when he was a child. He held this ideal unconsciously until he was in his late twenties, that is, through the first (meeting-and-formation) stage of his marital life cycle.

In telling his story, Wolfgang pointed out the origin of his ideal-mate image: "When my father's family moved to the States from Europe, he began to work so that he could go to college. His parents told him that if he gave them his checks, they would save the money for him and then pay for his college when the time came. However, when the time came, they had spent the money." Wolfgang drew from this story his ideal: someone who would not repeat the pattern his father experienced as a young adult. Instead, his ideal mate was someone who would ". . . mirror back to me love and acceptance. She would be someone who would take an interest in me and who would take my feelings seriously. She would be someone who would not abandon me physically or emotionally."

He believed that his father's experience negatively impacted his father's life and thus the ability of both of Wolfgang's parents to be present for him. His father ultimately could not support Wolfgang's efforts to make something of his own life. Wolfgang particularly felt that his father was not "there for him" in his young adult life. Neither parent provided emotional or financial support for his college or seminary work. He understood that what was going on was because his grandparents had disappointed his father; but even so he felt abandoned by his parents in the crucial transition into young adulthood.

Wolfgang married right after college. Almost immediately, his marriage ran into conflict. He discovered how big the discrepancy was between his ideal-mate image and his real mate. He wanted to go to seminary, but his wife had not finished her education, and she wanted him to postpone his career goals so that she could fulfill hers. Prior to their marriage, he had expected that she would be supportive of his career goals and continue to make his educational preparation central to their early life plans, and then resume her education later. When she insisted on immediately completing her education, it was a severe challenge to his belief that he had married an ideal mate. Just as his father had, he felt betrayed. The feelings surfaced again of how his parents had failed to support him. It was hard for him to separate his feelings of disappointment with his parents from those he felt with his wife. He had expected that his wife would provide the support his parents never gave him, and when she did not, he was devastated.

Here again, we see the influence of the traditional images of women and men coming through. He expected his wife to sacrifice her own needs of selfhood in favor of his needs.

Wolfgang also pointed out that his image of an ideal marriage was one where he and his wife would agree on everything. He felt abandoned when his wife expressed differences with him. It reminded him of the abandonment he had felt with his parents.

Wolfgang was in a lot of turmoil at the time of the retreat as he recalled the early days of his marriage. He and his wife managed to hold on to their mutual commitment and get through that period, but the issues had not been resolved. They both still had some bitter feelings. Wolfgang was forced to revise his ideal-mate and marriage images, but he had not really given up those ideals. They still exerted a mighty force within him.

At the time of the retreat, Wolfgang was not involved in the life of a congregation as a staff person. As a result he was able to devote much of his emotional energy to resolving the discrepancy between his ideal mate and real mate. He was able to attend seminary, carry on a part-time job, and support his wife's efforts to get her own education. Had he been in a local congregation as a staff member, the quality of his emotional investment in staff duties would have been severely impacted by his marital conflict.

The Myth of Repudiating Family-of-Origin Pitfalls

It is typical that we want to avoid the pitfalls and problems we witnessed in our family of origin. Therefore, at the conscious level we make an effort to marry someone who we believe can potentially help us avoid repeating the past. This is a common expectation for many religious caregivers.

The myth of repudiation is an ideal-mate image wherein we expect our mate to repudiate something of our negative family-of-origin experience. Our family-of-origin experience has been so negative that we not only want the positive experiences to be repeated but also want to avoid the repetition of the bad family patterns. It is intuitive that our desire to avoid the negative family-of-origin patterns is stronger than our desire to repeat the positive family experiences.

Esther was able to point out that her ideal-mate image was based on what she did *not* want in a mate rather than what she wanted. As a twenty-seven-year-old African American, she wanted her ideal mate not to be abusive, physically or emotionally, nor an alcoholic. She would never accept her mate cheating on her. Esther vowed never to accept someone less than her ideal.

Her ideal-mate image was, understandably, rooted in what she witnessed between her father and mother. Her father had many extramarital affairs, which Esther's mother told her about. Esther described her father, who did not deny his infidelities, as mean, self-centered, abusive, and self-hating. Understanding and knowing what her mother had to endure with her father, she did not want to repeat the same pattern in her own life. Esther said she'd rather stay single than go through what her mother did. Whenever a potential date even remotely reminded her of her father, she put a lot of distance between herself and the man.

Esther understood that she saw her father primarily through her mother's eyes. Because her mother expected her to side with her against her father, Esther grew concerned that she might not really know her father. She found the realization very intimidating. Esther's ideal was clearly reactive, rooted in her preoccupation with her parents' marital difficulties. As such, it was a negative expectation rather than a positive one.

On the positive side, however, Esther's experience moved her beyond traditional expectations of what it means to be a woman in marital and family relationships. She was critical of relationships where there was no mutuality between men and women, no sharing of responsibility for the relationship.

Esther was a seminary student preparing for ministry, and she was a student assistant to a local church. She was aware of the potential conflict she would face in ministry as a result of her problems around the ideal-mate image and the amount of time and energy she was putting into trying to reconcile her ideal image with her real mate. As the cases of Blake, Brenda, Wolfgang, and Esther show, how much of an emotional investment is available for caring depends on the extent to which the caregiver has reconciled ideal-mate images with the real mate. If we are not in a struggle to reconcile the images, we have more energy to invest in caregiving.

The Myth of the Knight in Shining Armor

When young girls are exposed to romantic stories, they often take root in their lives such that the girl, as she grows into adulthood, can draw on the stories at crucial points in her life cycle. Among the stories for young girls to choose from, the Cinderella and Sleeping Beauty myths are favorites. Women caregivers sometimes turn to these myths to help them face critical points of transition in their lives.

Yvonne said she had such a fairy-tale image of an ideal mate. She was African American and in her late twenties, a seminary student. Her marital myth was rooted in a belief that her prince would come (on a horse) and take her away one day and solve all her problems. Actually, the story of Sleeping Beauty was her favorite, with its deeply traditional notions of what it meant to be female.

When Yvonne was very young, she yearned to be special in the eyes of her parents. She found it hard to feel special because she always had to set aside her interests in order to be her parents' go-between. Like Esther, she saw marital strain between her parents, and again like Esther's parents they would put her in the middle of their problems. She felt torn between them and tried to mediate as a result. Resenting being used by her parents in this way, she vowed as a child that she would leave at the first chance. She coped with her parents' conflict by fantasizing that a prince in shining armor was coming to rescue her.

Her prince did come. She found him in college and married him. But as with all ideal-mate myths, she also encountered a real mate. He was not really the knight she expected, and that came as a disappointment to her. It was a novel discovery for her that marriage was real work. Coercing him into becoming her knight failed. Consequently, it took several years for her to reconcile her ideal mate with the real mate. Learning to accept his limitations and flaws was a real struggle for her.

Here again, in her professional life Yvonne was on the periphery of the church and did not have to make a large emotional investment in her caregiving. Instead, she expended her energies in the home, reconciling her ideal-mate and real-mate images.

The Myth of Unlimited Affection

Divorce and remarriage are common experiences among caregivers. Following divorce, the ideal-spouse image often resurfaces at the prospect of remarriage. It is not unusual for caregivers still to be struggling with ideal-mate images in the middle and late stages of the life cycle.

Kent was a middle-age white man who entered the ministry after forty. He was divorced, had several adult children, and was a grandfather. He had not remarried but had had several close relationships. He was determined not to settle for anyone less than ideal in remarriage. Kent had a definite ideal-mate image, relatively unchanged since early adulthood. He was still comparing potential mates to his ideal.

Kent's ideal-mate image epitomized definable, traditional female characteristics, which he articulated and ranked in order. At the top of the list was unlimited expression of affection toward him. By this he sought a mate who would give him kisses and hugs unselfishly and openly. Then, in descending order, he defined his ideal mate as intelligent, assertive, aggressive, self-actualized, self-differentiated, and having positive self-esteem.

We might think this wish list of characteristics is reasonable and realistic. It is, but somehow Kent always found potential mates who were undemonstrative and very needy emotionally. He seemed always to pick the ones who could not be or do what he thought he needed. The reason was that Kent was still reacting to his family-of-origin issues and unconsciously continuing to pick his mate based on a conflictual pattern from his relationship with his mother.

Kent's mother was a single parent who unconsciously drew him into the role that really belonged to his father. She made Kent her confidant and relied on him as other women would rely on a husband. Although Kent was very uncomfortable with that, he said he wanted to please his mother and be an obedient son. Looking back, he felt his mother had been so needy that he missed the love and nurture he needed as a child.

Kent unconsciously sought a mate who would not draw on him too much emotionally, as his mother had. He wanted more mutuality and did not want to be a caretaker for his mate. In adulthood, Kent felt trapped by his mother's expectations of him. He also felt abused by them and carried his resentment toward her. Kent was not, however, sufficiently self-differentiated from his mother to select a mate who could share affection mutually.

In Kent's abortive marriage, he played the caregiver and did the expressing of emotion, very much as he had with his mother. He said he was vulnerable to women who were emotionally needy and that he could not attract anyone emotionally self-differentiated. He hoped that one day he might find an ideal mate, or someone sufficiently close to the ideal who could express her affection without limit.

Kent was very vulnerable to being emotionally drained by his congregation. He was heavily committed to them, and people expected a lot out of him. Because he was still waiting for the ideal mate, his occasional relationships did not divert his emotional energy from the congregation. But the potential remained for conflict between the demands of the congregation and those of courtship and his deferred resolution of ideal- and real-mate images.

The Myth of Positive Communication

George and Shirley are both African American. They entered their marriage expecting not to repeat their negative family-of-origin patterns. Throughout a smooth courtship and engagement and the early stage of marriage, they felt they had done just that. They were totally unaware of the potential reenactment of negative family-of-origin dynamics.

Shirley had an absent father and thus sought a father figure in her husband. But when George acts fatherly, particularly in regard to decision making, she becomes very upset and rebellious. Because he is a father figure, she feels it's impossible to be direct and frank about what is on her mind. She either avoids what she wants to say or acts indirectly to get her point across.

George, too, grew up in a family where the man was missing. As the oldest child, he felt that his mother manipulated him a great deal to get him to do things. He felt she was not only manipulative but also deceitful and conniving. Thus when Shirley refuses to be direct, he grows very anxious and withdraws emotionally from her. This stimulates Shirley's feelings of abandonment, and a negative, escalating pattern of conflict develops.

Eventually both came to realize the pattern they were in, and they were able to identify its origins. Moreover, they identified their respective ideal-mate images at work in all the conflict. George's ideal mate would communicate frankly and openly no matter what the circumstances. Shirley's ideal mate would be present for her emotionally.

Aware of the nature and origins of their marital conflict, they know they do not have the ideal marriage they expected. For them, the ideal marriage is one in which conflict is short-lived and resolved reasonably quickly. They feel that in their marriage conflict goes on too long; they wonder whether they will ever overcome the problems facing them.

George and Shirley discovered their marital mythology and ideal images at a marital retreat that my wife and I led. Sometimes my wife and I spend extra time with couples who seem to have conflicting expectations; George and Shirley were such a couple. Their family-of-origin needs and conventional images of men's and women's roles were inseparable from their ideal images. They had to seek out the conflicting images and find a way to live with each other in harmony. To do so required them to reedit their marital ideal images.

Unlike the earlier cases we've seen, George puts a great deal of emotional effort into his church duties, and he resents having to spend so much time resolving issues at home. At the time of the retreat, he felt able to manage both sets of demand on his emotional energy.

The Myth of Limited Possibility in Midlife

I close this section on ideal-marriage images by exploring my own, because it illustrates another common marital myth: that change is not really possible in midlife.

As of June 1996, my wife and I have been married for thirty years. Both my parents are living with us. My mother is eighty-nine and my father ninety-one. They have been married for fifty-seven years. My mother-in-law is still alive and is eighty-three; my father-in-law has been deceased for more than ten years. My in-laws had been married for more than fifty years when my father-in-law died. I know of some of the struggles of both sets of parents. I feel they did not have perfect marriages, but I think their marriages were OK. I expect in my marriage what I saw in theirs. Thus, I have developed my images of the ideal marriage on what I perceived were realistic expectations in the parental marriages.

In the twenty-ninth year of marriage I came to realize that I had been doing a disservice to my wife and our marriage. I felt our struggles and problems could not be solved and would remain forever. Accepting what happiness we had achieved to that point, I felt we could go no further than our parents had.

This began to change, however. I saw that our parents had done the best they could, given the resources they had. The resources my wife and I had, however, were different. We had more than our parents had, and with those greater resources we could address the issues and problems pertinent to our marriage.

At midlife, the marital issues we thought we had dealt with earlier in the marriage began to resurface—particularly when my parents came into our home. I saw firsthand how hard it was for both my parents to be close with each other and expressive. In observing their patterns, I decided I could do much better about being close to my spouse than I had in the past. At that point, I saw another, hopeful way of relating in my own marriage.

For me, issues of closeness and intimacy followed the traditional lines of expectations of men and women. Men are not expected to do well in the area of intimacy, whereas women are supposed to be experts. Fortunately, I am revising my ideal self-image to include working on my own ability to be intimate.

These resurfacing issues had an impact on my ministry, but it was lessened because my wife and I were aware that the energy we were expending on our relationship could disrupt our teaching. Consequently, we sought therapeutic help to be sure we cared for ourselves and our marriage during this period, while keeping the same level of emotional availability in our work.

Family Myths

The Myth of Fulfilling the Family Legacy

It is time to explore family myths. Family myths are made up of ideal or perfect-child images. Each marital partner brings an image of the ideal child to the family, and it shapes the interaction between the couple and their children. The ideal-child image becomes the standard to which the growing child is held during the expansion phase of the family life cycle.

The Singleton family is African American. Mitchell, the father, is pastor of a local congregation; in their faith he and his wife, Nicky, are Pentecostal and evangelical. They had a young adult daughter and a teenage son at the time I first encountered them. Grace was the ideal child in the parents' minds, and she conformed very well to her parents' expectations. She was obedient, a hard-working student, and a well-rounded, good child who presented very few problems to her parents. As an adolescent, their son Clarence was the opposite of his sister and provided many sleepless nights to the Singletons.

When I met the Singletons, they were in the contraction phase of their life cycle, in which children leave home, and also preparing to launch their third and last child into the world. Their image of the ideal teenage child was grounded in their religious ideas. They believed in a patriarchal ideal: the eldest son should be dedicated to God for religious service. Approaching their middle years, they were concerned about the family legacy being passed on through their male child. They were very vocal in passing on this expectation to Clarence. He was told his elaborate birth mythology and how his life would be dedicated to God to carry on the family tradition of religious service. Every generation had had a minister, and they expected him to follow the tradition.

The older Clarence became, the more he rebelled against his parents' expectations. By sixteen, he did exactly the opposite of whatever was asked of him. He declared his right and need to live his own life. He engaged in criminal activities: stealing cars and selling drugs.

Of the parents, Nicky was the more upset by Clarence's behavior. Her own ideal-parent expectations seemed to be wrapped up in it. Nicky believed that her success as a parent rested on whether each child conformed to her ideal-child image. She was bitterly disappointed in Clarence because he made her feel she was a failure as a parent. To protect herself from being overwhelmed by her feelings of failure, she withdrew all affection from Clarence.

Mitchell was baffled by his son's attitude and behavior. He believed his son was going through a difficult phase of growing up; he wanted to be emotionally present for the boy. But he was terribly concerned about the criminal activity. Taking a wait-and-see attitude, he hoped that Clarence would eventually get through this phase of development successfully.

The Singletons were at different points of view on what to do with their son. Nicky made it clear she was letting Mitchell deal with him. This pleased Clarence and lessened the tension in the home. Clarence was determined to find his own niche in life, and he was not going to be forced to accept his parents' expectations for him.

During all this conflict, things were very difficult for Mitchell at the church. People were unhappy that he was not present for them as he once had been. They called the regional executive and expressed their dissatisfaction. Mitchell decided that he could not continue in the church, given the emotional demands being made by his son. He left the church and took a secular job where he could pay more attention to Clarence.

The Myth of Premature Adult Responsibility

The Houstons are white, married, and in their thirties. Believing that they needed to have their individual adult lives and careers well developed before marriage and starting a family, both first established successful careers in the work world. Blanton Houston is a clergyman, and Annette is an advertising consultant.

The Houstons were very deliberate in their plans for children. They knew exactly how many children they wanted: two. Their child-raising philosophy was intact, and they had verbalized their ideal-child expectations. Wanting to raise children who would be independent thinkers reasoning for themselves, they set out to train them not to blindly conform to the expectations of others. They believed in a participatory form of child raising wherein children were given the right to express their own opinions and participate in family discussions and decision making.

Brittany arrived when the Houstons were in their late thirties. Because of their ages, they decided not to have any more children.

Brittany was the ideal child and met those expectations until she was thirteen. As a budding adolescent, she began to rebel against everything that was expected of her. She began to have problems at school and at home. Brittany was no longer reasonable and refused to solve her problems in that way. What concerned her parents the most was that it became the norm for her to express hostility toward her parents, and her anger triggered her parents' anger. They were surprised at themselves and at their reaction to Brittany. Still, they desired to be the ideal, reasonable parents and so went on trying always to exhibit patience. The Houstons felt that if they continued to treat her as an adult, Brittany would eventually respond.

The more patience they exhibited, the worse Brittany became. They began to believe that she was not ready for adult responsibility, and that it was premature to expect this of her. Only when they came to that conclusion and began to respond to her in a more age-appropriate way did Brittany improve in her behavior at school and at home. The Houstons realized that expecting democratic participation was premature, and that Brittany would have to learn to be an adult gradually in keeping with her emotional and psychological readiness. She had been overwhelmed by the push for responsibility; she had to learn to be responsible in small steps.

The Houstons sought help early with Brittany. Consequently, Blanton's ministry felt minimal impact from his emotional travails at home. He did not have to withdraw at all from emotional availability at the church.

Negative Family Myths

The final section of this chapter deals with negative family myths: those of dire consequences, family mediation, and the scapegoat. These myths are natural outgrowths of accepting a rigid role within one's family of origin. While all three myths stem from the same family dynamics, we each live out the myth and experience the world differently. For example, in the myth of mediation a particular family member feels compelled to be the family reconciler because she is accustomed to having every family member turn to her when there is conflict. In the myth of the family scapegoat, a family member is selected to carry the whole family's pain and guilt, and he is blamed for all the family's problems. In the former case, the myth casts the person as a potential heroine; in the latter, he can do no right in the family's eyes. In the myth of dire consequences, one person feels compelled to play a certain "heroic" role in the family, as does the mediator, with the difference that in this myth the very survival of the family is dependent on this one person. The mediator is not saddled with the idea that family survival depends on her.

For caregivers, the danger of these negative family myths is that we tend to play the same roles in our caregiving that we play or played in our families of origin. We believe our emotional survival is at stake when we play out our family role expectations in our caregiving.

The Myth of Dire Consequences

This myth is a belief, shared by all family members, that the family cannot survive unless a selected person plays a specific—for him sacrificial—role. What makes the myth negative is just this need to sacrifice his own growth and development while actually thinking that the sacrifice is essential for the family to survive. This is often the case with caretakers who are expected to take on premature adult responsibility. The family as a whole believes that it cannot function well without that person performing this essential role.

As an example, consider a person who marries in order to escape the family-of-origin expectations. The family, however, never accepts the fact that the person is married, and at every opportunity members of the family of origin seek to undermine the marriage. In this particular case, she has a divided loyalty in that she feels torn between the expectations of the family of origin and the realistic demands of the marriage. It is hard for her to be self-differentiated from the family of origin in that she feels she can't leave the family and still keep family members happy.

I have encountered many religious caregivers over the years who were assigned burdensome roles in families where they were perceived to be essential to the family's survival. They are intimidated by thinking that the family will fall apart if they become self-differentiated. For example, I believed that my parents would not be able to get along after I left for college. I thought there would be dire consequences in my absence. I often worried about how they were going to make it in their marriage. They taught me a lesson, however. While their marriage still had conflict, they were able to survive quite well without me.

The Myth of the Family Mediator and the Myth of the Scapegoat

Closely related to the myth of dire consequences are these two equally negative myths. They, too, have consistent themes that I have seen in the lives of numerous religious caregivers. The myth of mediation finds a particular family member selected to be the family reconciler, to whom every family member turns when there is conflict. In the myth of the family scapegoat, the family member is selected by the family to carry its pain and guilt.

In terms of religious caregivers, the scapegoat feels guilty when he tries to self-differentiate and decides this is a sin against the family. (For the religious caregiver, the role of scapegoat takes on divine connotations and is enchained to the demands and needs of the congregational family—to the point that he will have to forgo self-differentiation and be blamed for other people's shortcomings.) He takes on the guilt if something happens to family members, and he is prone to give up the push for self-differentiation in order to make things better within the family. Feeling totally responsible for family-of-origin members, he is not free emotionally to enter other relationships outside that family. Members of the family of origin seek to keep him close; consciously or unconsciously, they blame him for family problems.

Marital and Family Mythologies and their Impact on Caregiving

Our expectations around images of the ideal mate, ideal child, ideal marriage, and ideal family all put pressure on us if there is any discrepancy between the ideal and the real. Resolving the conflict between ideal and real takes energy; as a result it can have an impact on our emotional presence in our caregiving.

Additionally, the ideal expectations that we bring to marriage and family life may be very similar to those we bring to relationships with parishioners and people for whom we care. As we have seen, unresolved family-of-origin issues are often transferred to the ideal mate or ideal child, who is then expected to make up for the deficits we sustained in our own early childhood. The same expectations can be transferred to caregiving settings, with the person receiving our care expecting us to make up for her own deficient childhood needs.

It is important for us to note that the transference can work in either direction, to or from the caregiver. Ideal expectations have an impact on both sides of ministry. Consider that in the myth of jubilation the ideal spouse is expected to make up for the lost childhood of the caregiver. The same expectation could come from those for whom we care.

Such expectations can go the other way, too. An example of the latter case is a pastor who might expect parishioners to accommodate his frequent trips out of town, on which he spends the church's money but does not feel he has to account for it. Such trips may in fact be principally for relaxation or pleasure and far exceed a normal allowance for vacation. It is as if the caregiver expects the congregation to provide for a lost childhood!

Another way that negative family and marital mythologies have an impact on our caregiving is in relationships. Sometimes those for whom we care get involved with us as the caregiver in a matchmaking process. Single caregivers are often warned to keep their dating outside of work settings, to avoid dual relationships. In a dual relationship, the caregiver relates to the receiver of care in multiple contexts where acceptable boundaries can easily be blurred. Sometimes the caregiver's own personal needs and myths push him into inappropriate involvements, where those in need of care are expected to meet the needs of the caregiver.

It has also been pointed out that what happens in the family of the caregiver impacts other family systems, particularly within churches and close communities (Friedman, 1985). The marital and family myths of the caregiver and those of the close community interact in complex and subtle ways. How many times have we heard it said that the minister's children are the worst children in town? Both the congregation and the pastor's family have ideal-child expectations to which the child alternately conforms or rebels. Thus, the congregation and the caregiving parents form a coalition that reinforces each party's ideal-child expectations. In such an environment, the child's needs often get overlooked. The point to be made is that as caregivers we need to recognize how our myths impact greatly what we do in both family and caregiving contexts. Consequently, it is crucial for us to attend to these caregiver's myths.

In addition to caregivers transferring expectations onto those in need of caregiving, there are also expectations from those who receive care. There are two "nonnegotiable" expectations that people usually have of religious caregivers: (1) we must be superhuman, and (2) for those of us who are ministers, the minister and his or her family must be models or exemplars of superior behavior and impeccable living for the entire community (Wimberly and Wimberly, n.d.; Mace and Mace, 1980). Given these expectations, there are certain myths that impact how we function as minister or caregiver. Perhaps the most influential is the family myth of dire consequences, in which we feel that we are absolutely indispensable for everything in the church to work; if we don't do our job, everything will fall apart. I often hear caregivers say how surprised they are when they discover the church functioned better during their illness than when they were healthy and available! In other words, our need to be needed can get in the way of the development of lay leadership.

Summary

This chapter presents many common myths that appear in the married and family lives of religious caregivers. The catalogue of myths included here is, again, not exhaustive. As with the personal myths found in Chapter Two, these family and marital myths vary with the individual, depending on the themes present in the life experiences of the person(s) involved.

The significance of marital and family myths is that all marriages and families have them. The more mature and self-differentiated adult family members are, the better able they are to revise these myths to deal with the marital and family realities. When marital partners and adult family members are able to revise their marital and family myths as a means of negotiating discrepancies between ideal images and real persons and situations, the myths can become nurturing and sustain the growth and development of family members. The opposite is the case when marital partners and adult family members are not able to revise their myths to deal with marital and family realities.

In this chapter, we have treated as synonymous the notions of *perfection* and *ideal* as we look at caregiver's images of family and marriage. The myth of perfection has an indissoluble relationship to each myth presented in this chapter.

MARITAL AND FAMILY MYTHOLOGY QUESTIONNAIRE

Because our emotional investments must be shared between the different families in which we are involved (family of origin, family of creation, family of the church), it is important for us to begin to explore the various levels of our marital and family myths. A sure way of knowing when our different myths are actively working is when we notice that people in the different families are expressing disappointment or dissatisfaction with us. This could come from our spouses, our children, our parishioners, or our careseekers. Often, the complaints have to do with the degree to which we invest ourselves emotionally in them, and whether we maintain that level of involvement and presence for them.

How we respond to their disappointment is influenced greatly by the myths that are operating in our lives. The more we can identify the different myths that are at work, the better we can respond to the disappointment others project upon us. The key is having enough emotional energy for the different families in which we are involved, and learning how our myths operate in our lives can help us be better caregivers and people.

You may now want to begin discovering your own marital and family myths. The following questions can assist in this process.

EXERCISE I Attending to the Ideal-Mate Image and the Real Mate

1. Think about your earliest images of what you wanted in a mate. What was or is your ideal-mate image? Identify his or her characteristics and qualities.

2. What events or situations contributed to the development of your image of the ideal mate?

3. How have the actual mates in your life conformed to your ideal-mate images? Include friendships and dating partners as well as actual marital partner(s) (if you are married).

4. How have you tried to negotiate the discrepancies between the ideal and the real? Have you tried to force your mate into your ideal image, or have you accepted your mate as he or she is? How long have you been trying to negotiate these discrepancies?

EXERCISE II   Ideal Marriage and Real Marriage

1. Identify your earliest image of what an ideal marriage would be.

2. What events or situations contributed to the development of your ideal image of marriage?

3. How have your actual marriage and your ideal-marriage image compared?

4. How have you tried to negotiate the discrepancies between the ideal and the real? How long have you been engaged in this process? What have the results been so far?

EXERCISE III   Ideal Family/Child and Real Family/Child

1. Identify your earliest ideal image of a family.

2. What events or situations contributed to the development of your ideal image of the family?

3. How have your family of creation and your ideal image compared with each other?

4. How have you tried to deal with the discrepancies between them? How long have you been engaged in this process?

5. What is your ideal-child image? What events or situations contributed to the development of your ideal-child image?

6. How have you tried to negotiate the differences between the ideal and the real?

EXERCISE IV   Changes in Ideal-Family Image

1. Revisit your ideal family image.

2. What experiences and people contributed to this ideal image?

2. How has this image changed over the years?

3. How has this image influenced your present life?

EXERCISE V   Ideal-Parent Image

1. What is your ideal of the perfect parent?

2. What experiences and people helped you form this ideal?

3. How has this image changed over the years? If you are a parent, how did becoming a parent change your ideal-parent image?

4. How has this image influenced your present life?

EXERCISE VI   Negative Family Myths

1. Are there things in the past of your family of birth (or family of origin) that you and other family members want to forget or hide from yourselves? Examples might be abortion, extramarital affair, prison record, out-of-wedlock birth, unconventional sexual activity, or extreme family conflict.

2. What mechanisms have you and your family of origin used to hide, forget, or deny these problems or not face them? Here are possible mechanisms:

Paint a rosy but distorted picture of the family (this could be considered a myth of family harmony)

Blame one family member for all of the family's problems (the myth of the scapegoat)

Restrict each family member's behavior to a prescribed, inflexible role, while promoting the belief that deviation from that role (that is, individuality or self-differentiation) might cause other, serious harm (this could be called a myth of catastrophe)

Avoid all family conflict, in the belief that real families have no conflict or disagreements (a myth of pseudomutuality)

Deny or evade one another, or placate a family member, to avoid admitting there are any problems, in the belief that the family must appear united at all costs (a myth of togetherness)

Foil the possibility that an outsider will enter the family, by marriage or otherwise, and save the family from having to deal with its problems (a myth of salvation and redemption)

ASSESSMENT

1. What are the dominant themes and subthemes that are apparent in your view of the ideal-mate, ideal-child, ideal-family, and negative family myths? For example, are certain gender-related themes evident? Are there themes related to the public image of the family?

Can you and your family of origin face the truth about yourselves, or do you have to hide the truth?

2. Trace the influence of these themes across several previous generations: parents, grandparents, great-grandparents.

3. If you are married, how are these themes visible in the way you relate to your family of creation and in the lives of your offspring?

4. If you are remarried following divorce or the death of a spouse, trace the influence of the themes in each family context.

5. Compare the ideal expectations you brought to marriage and the expectations you bring to your relationships with parishioners and others whom you care for. Identify the myth(s) explored in this chapter that have affinity to the one(s) you hold. Describe those elements with which you have the greatest affinity. Examine how these elements have had or are now having an impact on how you relate in your family and caregiving contexts.

·4

MINISTRY MYTHS

STORIES THAT HELP OR HINDER US
IN SERVING GOD

THERE COMES A TIME when ministers question or have reservations about full commitment to ministry. It is my experience that this reservation comes from an inner emotional and spiritual struggle related to mythologies about the ministry. These myths comprise certain themes, often dealing with unresolved issues coming from formative experiences and family-of-origin patterns, specifically those of premature adult responsibility.

Caregivers who take on premature adult responsibility are often victims of ideal or perfect-child expectations. They become overfunctioners and take on the major responsibility for maintaining and cultivating relationships. They learn to neglect their own needs, repress deep resentments about being taken for granted by others, and seek caring roles as a way to deal with and medicate their hurts and unreturned love. They often seek relationships that perpetuate their family-of-origin roles; close relationships are a frustrating and unrewarding experience. Likewise, relationships within the ministerial setting are felt to be extremely threatening. In short, many caregivers who come to spiritual renewal retreats, pastoral counseling, and seminary are the walking wounded, whose need for relief from overwhelming roles is very acute.

In this chapter, we look at the central ministerial myth of "overfunctioning," its origins in early childhood experiences and peer relationships, and the cultural influences helping to shape it. Then we examine related myths:

○ The myth of self-sufficiency
○ The myth of the underfunctioner
○ The myth of sacrificing joy
○ The myth of pleasing at all costs

These major myths are accompanied by related themes: resentment, searching for intimacy, inability to have fun, hurting people because of one's wounds, and unforgiveness. Once again, the myth of perfect empathy seems to be the background ideal that informs much of the overfunctioning that plagues ministers.

The Nature of Ministerial Myths

The sources of ministerial mythology range from the religious caregiver's private inner life to a sense of calling, to family roles and dynamics, to religious upbringing, to theological and ecclesiastical traditions, and to sociocultural roles.

Diverse, interrelated themes make up a ministerial mythology: the call, self-esteem, self-differentiation, social roles, authority, and narrative plots. The call relates to our awareness that a form of ministry or vocation will be our life's work. Self-esteem affects how we feel about ourselves, particularly our feelings of being valued, loved, and cared for (Satir, 1972, 1967). Self-differentiation is the ability to take the "I" position in the context of family, that is, the maturity and ability to know who we are apart from others (Bowen, 1978; Kerr and Bowen, 1988). Social roles are understood as the sociocultural expectations that inform our attitudes, knowledge, and behavior (Hunter, 1990). Authority deals with influence over others and using this influence positively or negatively (Malony and Hunt, 1991). Finally, literary plots are creative configurations and the ordering of different themes within the ministerial mythology that give overall meaning and direction to our lives as caregivers.

In summary, ministerial mythologies are interrelated themes that form a comprehensive image of ministry; the themes often have "plots" that we live out in our work as caregivers. Frequently, these plots reveal a comprehensive vision of ministry and are expressions of a vibrant, healthy, and mature self that has a good balance between meeting the needs of self and of others. Sometimes, however, the plots express a poor and depleted self that lacks that healthy balance. Helping religious caregivers identify these themes and the images of ministry that they articulate is an essential part of the spiritual renewal process.

The Myth of Overfunctioning

Overfunctioning is very common among religious caregivers. We are quite prone to the conviction that we must take on the major responsibility for maintaining and enhancing relationships with others. Overfunctioning is both a role and a myth. It has the function of a role in that we carry it out. It is a myth because we believe that we must play this role in order to be fulfilled in life.

The concept of the overfunctioner as a role was made popular by Edwin H. Friedman in his well-known book *Generation to Generation: Family Process in Church and Synagogue* (1985). To Friedman, overfunctioning is a role assigned to a family member (or members) in which he is only valued if he performs a certain role. We might have assumed the role in our families if there was a lot of anxiety and we took on the responsibility to lessen it for the family. We behave responsibly, but we take on so much extra responsibility that we rob others of the opportunity to exercise normal responsibility, with the result that people around us become underfunctioners. In short, what appears to be responsible behavior is in fact inappropriate behavior.

We can infer overfunctioning as a myth from Friedman's thought. It is more than just a role we play; it is a conviction about our lives and our ministry. As a myth, it has an underlying narrative that informs behavior. In overfunctioning behavior, the narrative says our lives have no meaning unless we are working hard to make sure that others fulfill their lives.

When the overfunctioning role is assigned by the family, it is irrational and develops very early. This is called "parentification" of children, in which parents abdicate their responsibility and assign the family's caring tasks to their children (Nichols, 1984). This role assigning by parents or significant others represents ideal or perfect-child expectations. Of course, a young child has difficulty negotiating these early demands; the expectations are internalized and become part of the child's self-understanding.

James Framo calls parentification premature assignment of adult responsibility; he uses the concept of irrational role assignment to describe it (Framo, 1972). The role assignment is irrational because it has demands and expectations associated with the child's grandparents. That is, parents expect their children to take the place of the grandparents and to perfectly make up for what they (the child's parents) missed when they were children. Moreover, the role assignment is dangerous because it exploits the child and disconfirms her identity. It sets the stage for a variety of later personality problems, one of which is being an overfunctioner in caregiving relationships. Caregivers who have been "parentified" often feel trapped in nonproductive roles. They are angry at being used, are unable to relinquish control, and feel devalued.

Overfunctioning in relationships is also a gender expectation for women in Western culture. The traditional expectation of women is to function well in all things, whether at home or in the workforce, and to take primary responsibility for maintaining relationships (Taylor, Gilligan, and Sullivan, 1995; Moessner and Glaz, 1991; and Gill-Austern, 1996). It is the image of the "superwoman."

It is not unusual to find men and women overfunctioners in ministry. Because of our family-of-origin role assignments as well as such tradition-bound cultural expectations, as religious caregivers we find it easy to overfunction.

Buster was a forty-year-old black from one of the Caribbean islands. He was conceived six months after the loss of a sibling in childbirth. His parents were overjoyed by his birth; he recalled that his birth brought happiness into the home. He grew into the role of bringing joy to the family. But his father died when he was a teenager. Although he was the fourth child, at that critical time the family looked to him to bring peace and return stability to the family. In effect, he became the family minister.

Buster overfunctioned in his family role for a long time. But he could point to one experience in clinical pastoral education in seminary that made him aware of his overfunctioning role:

> Many times I have found myself doing someone else's job. I have always had to do my work and take responsibility for my life. In fact, one of the major issues I had to wrestle with in my CPE was caretaking for other people. Overextending myself in doing things for people that they could do for themselves was my role. I am still working on this issue even now.

He continues, exploring where he first found the motivation for confronting his overfunctioning pattern:

> In my tenure in CPE, I was called to the room of a man where the family had given permission to the doctors to pull the plug from life support systems. This man's illness was due to overworking, by doing two jobs most of his life. He was an African American, age forty-three, who suffered a stroke that led to internal bleeding. His family complained about his not slowing down. This experience frightened the hell out of me because in 1987 I too suffered a stroke. I was working, studying, and preaching nightly for three months. I am blessed to still be alive.

Buster realized that overfunctioning could have serious results. This is the case for most of us, of course. While overfunctioning helps us achieve our ministerial goals in life, the costs for our emotional and physical well-being can be too high.

In addition to the emotional and physical toll, negative results are clear when we explore how overfunctioning affects others. Friedman points out that whenever there is an overfunctioner, there has to be an underfunctioner (1985). As an adaptive response, overfunctioning inevitably restores balance in human relationships. In a time of emphasis upon enabling lay leadership within local churches, ministerial overfunctioning could obstruct our efforts to equip the laity.

Common Ministerial Myths

The Myth of Self-Sufficiency

The larger myth of overfunctioning is home to the theme of self-sufficiency. Those of us who are loners and remain aloof are quite vulnerable to this myth, the belief that we are self-sufficient and don't need anyone else in performing our ministerial roles. Customarily, the person visualizes himself as being already perfect. Of course, this self-deception was nurtured in childhood. The belief of self-sufficiency develops in those of us who generally were overfunctioners as children and were given unusual control and leadership in our families of origin. Often, we were assigned adult responsibility prematurely, but we were very successful in pulling it off. That early success in fulfilling adult role expectations led to a self-deceptive sense of perfection.

Catherine is an African American minister who was raised by her grandmother. Her grandmother was very sick during most of Catherine's childhood. Being alone most of the time, since her parents allowed her to live with her grandmother, she was the woman's sole caretaker. She cooked for her, bathed her, paid her bills, and made sure someone was there to care for her when she was not home. All this took place while Catherine was preadolescent.

Not only did this family-of-origin assignment shape her role with her grandmother and later her understanding of ministry, but cultural gender factors were also formative. Catherine's call to the ministry came in her forties, after she had been in the business world for many years. She was extremely successful in the corporate world, where her independence and autonomy—which she developed as a child—facilitated her ascent of the corporate ladder. It appears she was also influenced, probably unknowingly, by the superwoman image that was then emerging but is now prevalent in society (Taylor, Gilligan, and Sullivan, 1995).

The superwoman sees herself as independent, self-sufficient, and able to manage everything by herself. She is the new cultural ideal, but it is one whose primary quality is total independence from people. The superwoman is a woman without relationships. As an ideal that requires separation from self as well as from others, it presents a dangerous pattern to follow (Taylor, Gilligan, and Sullivan, 1995; Miller-Mclemore, 1991).

While the ideal focuses primarily on white middle-class women, research reveals that many African American girls and women are well aware of it (Taylor, Gilligan, and Sullivan, 1995). Many African American teenagers are planning to follow this image of the ideal woman in their future, the research suggests.

The tradition of the African American matriarch is a historic legacy that emphasizes the strength of African American women. According to Teresa E. Snorton, the image of "womanist" has replaced the negative notion of the black matriarch, emphasizing the strength of African American women (Snorton, 1996). *Womanist* emphasizes resilience, strength, independence, and adaptation to deep disappointments in life.

African American women have often had to face adversity without recourse to being vulnerable. In fact, Snorton says, many were taught that they had to expect the worst, surrender to God, spare the feelings of others, and affirm their strength in the community of faith. A strong woman did not feel fear, sadness, or dread. She just kept her feelings to herself in order to spare others. In Snorton's mind, expressing feelings of vulnerability would set her outside and against the community.

Snorton goes on to say that there must be a safe place for "the womanist to express her deeper feelings without having to give up her strength and without feeling too vulnerable" (1996, p. 60). Vulnerability is risky for the womanist, who must contend with sexism, racism, and classism. This is because too much self-focus might erode the womanist's capacity for survival in a hostile world.

It is not clear that Catherine was influenced by the superwoman or womanist images. However, more and more female religious caregivers have to go it alone in their ministries because of lack of support and because there are so many people out there who prefer self-sufficient overfunctioners in ministry. That is to say, there are those who will let others do all the work. There are also those who don't want women in ministry and will do all they can to hinder women's progress (Glover-Wetherington, 1996).

Cultural images of what is masculine often influence men as well. To be masculine has customarily meant being self-sufficient and going it alone without support or help from others.

Self-esteem depends on having relationships with others in which we are neither overly engaged nor overly distant. Connecting with others

helps us foster self-esteem, while withdrawing from relationships under-
mines self-esteem and sets us up to be victims of our own negative inner
life and negative internalizations. Self-condemnation comes as a result of
internalized negative relationships that we have sustained in our early life;
they take on voices in our minds that condemn us and our behavior. Withdrawing intensifies such voices, such that they are almost impossible to
overcome unless we are engaged in positive relationships with others.

The real impact of this myth is that it separates men and women from
their true selves. Interconnectedness, mutuality, and interdependence are a
more fitting approach to ministry, for both sexes; they are essential for
our selfhood (Moessner, 1991). Pursuing self-sufficiency in ministry is self-
suicide, a far cry from and contrary to caring for oneself.

The Myth of Sacrificing Joy

There is a long tradition of self-sacrifice in Western and European Chris-
tianity. Part of this tradition is a negative attitude toward worldly pleasures and joy. To be a sad Christian is to be marked as someone special
in the Kingdom of God. Because of the prominence of self-sacrifice in
Western and European theology, many ministers are prone to developing
myths where denial of worldly pleasures is the norm. The theology of
denial of joy, when combined with family-of-origin dynamics, has considerable negative consequences for us religious caregivers.

Mark is African American. He was concerned that he deeply resented
his adolescent children having fun. He said that he had become a killjoy
in the home, and that his children and wife were getting tired of him. He
wanted desperately to alter his way of living.

As a youth, Mark did the caretaking for alcoholic parents, thus sacrificing his childhood. He believed that his resentment of his children went
back to his early childhood and teenage years, when he always had to be
doing adult things for his parents.

The myth of sacrificing joy is the belief that having fun is frivolous and
a waste of time when one could be doing much more with life. Sacrifice
of fun and joy is rooted not only in family-of-origin dynamics but also in
the cultural and historical legacy of capitalism in Europe and the United
States. The religious roots of capitalism grew out of Calvinism and
Lutheranism in Europe and were transported to the North American
colonies by Puritanism. An important conviction in this legacy was that
one should avoid sin through work and involvement in serious, work-
related pursuits. Serious work was a way to perfection: "The individual
must control and repress whatever in him reflects the world's sinfulness

and corruption: any tendency to engage in effort only in spurts, and then slacken; any complacent treatment of past attainments as ends in themselves; and spontaneous unreflected attachment to familiar, comfortable, emotionally gratifying arrangements; any carefree enjoyment of the present for its own sake; any reliance for guidance in his conduct on unreflecting feeling or unexamined routine; any temptation to blame his own failing on circumstances or fate rather than his own inadequacies" (Poggi, 1983, p. 68).

The repression of joy that is reflected in this Calvinist statement still has a great deal of influence in the religious and secular community in the United States. It is also a major influence in racial and class stereotypes regarding group laziness, extending to politics and welfare reform on the contemporary scene. Consequently, it is clear how pervasive is the influence of the sacrifice of joy as a central ingredient to being considered a success in North American society. Everyone in contemporary society knows the myth of sacrifice of joy at some level, because it is transmitted through a variety of channels of communication in our culture. Mark, then, had the sanctioned support of the religious and work beliefs of his community when he chose to sacrifice joy.

The impact on the caregiver is an overemphasis on the merits of law as opposed to grace. The caregiver tends to favor the letter of the law, right procedures, planning, and organization rather than process and the relationships involved in accomplishing activities. We take a no-nonsense stance at every opportunity, even when some levity and fun could facilitate accomplishing goals.

The Myth of Pleasing at All Costs

It sounds ironic, but the myth of pleasing is related to the theme of self-sacrifice. We often sacrifice who we are to make sure that others are happy; we place their need for nurture and growth before our own. The desire to please and be liked becomes so overwhelming at times that we literally lose our sense of self. As caregivers, we are prone to living out this myth.

In exploring her ministerial mythology, Ruby, an African American in her mid-thirties, encountered the theme of pleasing. She was an overfunctioner, with that role relating to her need to please. She believed she would be happy by pleasing people; if she did not please, dire consequences would result. She supposed that her salvation lay in the perfection of pleasing.

She attracted and dated men who were unable to take full responsibility for their own lives; she tried to please them by being responsible in their place. As a result, she would feel used and unappreciated. This feeling of being abused became a major theme and conflict for her, and a source of great concern.

Ruby's problem stemmed from "catastrophic expectations," the fear that drastic consequences will come if we do not do certain things that others expect of us (Corey, 1991). It is the cognitive belief that our lives will be meaningless and empty if we do not fulfill such expectations. This intimidation propels us into ritualistic, repetitive, self-deprecating behaviors. The fear comes from our view that people would not like us if they saw the real us. Ruby believed she could survive only if she hid her real self from others and accommodated others' wishes. She concluded that she should reach out and care for others so they would not see who she really was.

Feeling that others would not be interested in her own problems and concerns, Ruby minimized them. Denying her vulnerability and the hurt she felt inside, she never let others see her inner pain. She did not want to be a burden to others; she feared that being a liability might drive others away. In a word, she lived as if to be herself would mean isolation, loneliness, and pain. Her catastrophic fear was that to be herself would bring a kind of death.

Research shows that there is a crucial time in the life of every young girl, regardless of race, when she decides whether to sacrifice her sense of self in order to get along in relationships. At adolescence a shift takes place, particularly among middle-class girls. They force themselves to be silent, in conformity to the dominant images of what it means to be feminine and mature women. Some African American girls, notably from lower socioeconomic backgrounds, consciously rebel against being silent, but middle-class African American girls generally adopt a deliberate silence. There is considerable pressure on adolescent girls and young adult women, regardless of race, to sacrifice self for the sake of being a woman and catching a man.

Women are considered acceptable as caregivers if they are nice and not too threatening. This early, cultural pressure not to be oneself continues into adulthood and caregiving. The risk that the woman runs is loss of self and continuing depression, a devaluing of the person (Neuger, 1991). It is important that women caregivers feel free to be themselves, to assure their own mental and spiritual health as well as that of the people they care for.

Men also fall under the influence of the myth of pleasing. As for women, it usually takes the form of sacrificing self to win friends and be liked. Culturally, however, we men are expected to be able to live without the support and sanctions of others. It is "unmasculine" to be intimidated by the need to please others. As men, we too run the danger of caring to the neglect and loss of our own sense of self. Burnout and resentment are major casualties of the myth of pleasing.

The Myth of Underfunctioning

As we saw in exploring the myth of overfunctioning, overfunctioners produce the opposite effect in others by way of an inevitable balancing of the relationship. Where there is an overfunctioner, there must be an underfunctioner.

Underfunctioning can also arise from a belief that one is a victim. Thus it does not result only from being around an overfunctioner; underfunctioning can come from having significant others around who function minimally.

The theme in this ministerial mythology is a belief that we have no real capacity for ministry because of our victimization in childhood. Victimization arises from the blurring of boundaries between parent and child, where the parent fails to respect the parent-child relationship (Doehring, 1995).

Ricardo, a Hispanic in his late thirties, had a father who was violently abusive toward him. His father also failed to protect him from exploitation by the police; Ricardo went to prison for two years for a crime that his father committed. Punched and kicked whenever his father got drunk, Ricardo developed deep resentment and hatred toward him.

While in prison, Ricardo received a call to the ministry. He took it seriously; after serving his sentence he finished college and seminary. But Ricardo had never really come to grips with what his father had done to him. He secretly believed that he really did not have anything to offer to ministry because of his abusive treatment at the hands of his father. He came to our retreat hoping for some way out of his inability to deal with his history around his father.

Ricardo was also an underfunctioner in his family of creation. He felt entitled in marriage and expected his wife to provide what his parents had been unable to give him. His mother was physically abused by his father, and she provided very little support or protection for him. Ricardo expected absolute support from his wife regardless of his own inadequacies in their relationship. He was especially isolated from his teenage son, and verbally abusive to him. But Ricardo failed to make a connection between how he treated his teenage son and how his father had treated him. He had internalized his father's abusive personality.

Ricardo had real gifts for ministry. He was an excellent speaker, and he could minister effectively to those not part of his nuclear family. He successfully maintained a caring and supportive posture in his ministry. But inside, he suffered from festering anger and hostility toward authority and his father. He thought that spiritual renewal might bring some relief; a group of fellow pastors who knew Ricardo's story encouraged him to come to our retreat.

Unforgiveness became a major theme in Ricardo's myth of underfunctioning not because he should have forgiven his father, but rather because he failed to recognize that he had become like his father in how he treated his own family. Unforgiveness, then, relates to holding on to past resentments, to the extent that they hinder our ability to function appropriately in current relationships. One reason for holding onto past resentments and not coming to grips with them is that the powerless find power in refusing to forgive or let go (Patton, 1985). The abused are often powerless, at least at the time of the abuse; but holding on to resentments and hatred toward abusers helps give the abused a sense of power.

Ricardo's ministerial mythology was grounded in a belief that he was inadequate and flawed as a person. He felt somehow entitled to receive reparations from others for the sins his father had committed against him. He did not expect his parishioners to be the ones to make reparations, but he did treat his family that way—and those who got close to him. Still, there was a danger that eventually he might come to view his parishioners as benefactors who "owed" him reparations. Ricardo was an underfunctioner with the potential of drawing parishioners into his need for reparations.

A secondary mythology is evident in Ricardo's story: the myth of entitlement. This is the conviction that we are deserving of rewards because of our childhood victimization. In ministry, this might mean we expect to receive something tangible for past sacrifices (recognition of our saintliness) in the expectation that we no longer have to do anything to earn the rewards ("I've paid my dues").

Ricardo also ran into cultural images of what it means to be a man. Frequently, we who feel handicapped because of unfortunate circumstances in life are convinced that we cannot meet expectations surrounding manhood. Therefore, we must somehow be "compensated" for those circumstances before we can fully accept the role of manhood. Minority status in the United States contributes greatly to this belief. Nonetheless, in general men who feel flawed insist on compensation or reparations for their victimization before they can assume their rightful place as men. Ricardo was one man who felt that way.

Women can be underfunctioners, but in Western culture the powerful expectation that women take the major responsibility for relationships makes it difficult for them to fall back on any underfunctioning role. Doing so carries a great deal of negative sanction.

Summary

This chapter presents significant ministerial myths that are fairly common and to which many religious caregivers are prone. They arise from family-of-origin dynamics as well as from cultural images. Case vignettes offer illustrations of how these dynamics follow caregivers into their adult lives, as well as suggesting how lesser and related myths readily connect around caregiving. Many ministers have had conflictual childhoods, and their childhoods make them vulnerable to certain myths. This fact does not invalidate the call, however. Coming to grips with one's childhood difficulties and tending to the wounds caused by them become important sources of care for others. Moreover, we religious caregivers are well suited to be ministers despite our wounded childhoods because we are pushed into becoming responsible and effectively attaining adulthood prematurely. In addition, we seek to be in ministry not because of our childhood roles but rather because of a sense of calling, one that transcends our early vulnerabilities.

MINISTERIAL MYTHOLOGY QUESTIONNAIRE

This questionnaire is designed as a beginning for your reauthoring of your own ministerial mythology.

EXERCISE I   Call

1. Recall when you first became aware that a form of ministry would be your life's task. Where were you? Who else was there? What was said, and by whom? Whom did you tell about your decision? How did you feel?

2. Is your first awareness still a major motivating factor in your ministry today?

3. Does your call still sustain you today?

4. Does your call seem so far away that it has no real impact on your ministry?

EXERCISE II   Self-Esteem

1. Do you feel you can put the needs of others first in yo

2. Do you feel devalued when others' needs come before

3. Do you feel you have found a good balance between having your needs met and meeting the needs of others?

EXERCISE III   Self-Differentiation

1. Is it difficult to be yourself when you are around others?

2. Do you feel you have to conform to the expectations of others to be loved or accepted?

3. Can you assert who you are when there are costs to pay in doing so?

EXERCISE IV   Roles

1. Do you ever feel you are doing someone else's job?

2. Do others always do your work and take responsibility for your life?

3. Do you feel as if you pull your own weight?

4. Do you feel that you pull your weight and others' weight as well?

EXERCISE V   Authority

1. When you are around authority figures, do you feel you have to give in to them all the time?

2. Do you feel pressure to defend yourself or your position constantly around authority figures?

3. When you are around authority figures, do you find that most of the time you want to fight or contest things?

4. Are you able to articulate your position and values when they differ from those held by authority figures?

EXERCISE VI   Plots

1. Do you feel your life has purpose and is moving in a meaningful direction in your current ministry?

2. Do you feel trapped, that you are going nowhere in your current ministry?

SSESSMENT

1. Summarize the key themes that you see operating in your ministerial mythology.

2. What is the influence that these themes have had on your life?

3. What themes seem to need to be addressed in your ministry mythology?

4. How does your call address these themes?

5. Where would you place yourself on a continuum running from "walking wounded" to "wounded healer?"

6. Can you discern God's presence and help in addressing your themes?

7. What future goals can you set to deal with these themes?

8. Trace the influence of these themes back to the lives of parents, grandparents, and great-grandparents.

9. Can you see the influence of these themes in your offspring?

5

THE POSSIBILITY OF CHANGE

REAUTHORING THE MYTHS THAT BIND US

REAUTHORING IS ABOUT CHANGE in the personal, marital-family, and ministry myths. We can transform the beliefs and convictions we have long held about our sense of self, ourselves in relation to others, and how we engage in the activity of caring. Reauthoring recognizes that change in convictions and beliefs is possible; we are not totally at the mercy of our early childhood experiences, unconscious processes, and cultural conventions. While altering our myths is a slow process with much struggle and resistance, reauthoring moves forward as our resolve grows that we are neither totally passive in creating and formulating myths nor acquiescent in living out the stories that myths entail.

Myths are not just handed down. We play an active part in developing the myths that inform our lives. We have the capacity to interpret events and give them meaning and significance. As White and Epston (1990) put it, "In regard to family therapy . . . rather than proposing that some underlying structure or dysfunction in the family determines the behavior and interactions of family members, [the interpretive method] would propose that it is the meaning that members attribute to events that determines their behavior" (p. 3). Myth making, then, assumes that we are not powerless, not without agency in shaping the myths that inform our lives. We are participants in "meaning making" and story creating. Within realistic limits, it is possible to take responsibility for how we interpret reality and give meaning to it. Therefore, to some degree it is possible to alter the stories and myths that inform our behavior.

This chapter is about the possibility of changing personal, marital-family, and ministry myths. First, I identify the phases of the reauthoring process. I present a description of each phase, along with some idea of the personal work involved, what the experience of modifying myths is like at each phase, how difficult transformation is, the length of time change takes, how we move from one phase to the next, and how the process might have an impact on our lives and our ministry.

Some Assumptions About Reauthoring

Several significant assumptions underlie the reauthoring process:

1. Reality is socially constructed.
2. Transformation is possible, but not easy.
3. Change occurs normally throughout life cycle transitions, as well as at less predictable moments such as a sudden upheaval or trauma.
4. Innovation is facilitated when we can envisage our own role in creating our own myths.
5. Re-storying or discovering novel dimensions of our own stories facilitates transformation.
6. Bringing new perspectives to past experience helps create new story possibilities.

Transformation Is Possible

Myths can change, because they are inherently social constructions or social attributions (Berger and Luckman, 1966). Attribution assigns meanings to experience; attribution is shared as well as private. As we participate in life, we engage in attributing or assigning meaning, which gives significance to our experience. Early in our childhood, we must rely on publicly shared attributions common to our family and community. As we mature and grow older, however, we discover that unique and personal attributions are not only possible but can be different from those shared by others. Ultimately, as adults we combine shared and private attributions to shape our understanding of reality and experience.

Personal, marital-family, and ministerial myths are shared and private attributions in a storied formulation, a mythical pattern. They develop socially and personally, based on interactions with others as we participate in life. As social creations, myths are not just socially inherited or passed on to others without being personally modified. In fact, we make subtle shifts in them as we develop our own private attributions. All of this is to say that attributions that make up myths can be altered; they are modifiable in their evolution.

Transformation of Myths Is Difficult

While transformation is inherent to the formulation of myths, it is not always easy. Myths function to interpret reality and events that take place throughout life. In the early process of myth formulation, our experiences in the family of origin and with significant others are very influential—so influential that the myths evolved from them seem unalterably resistant to change. They seem to be part of an indelible, genetic blueprint, non-malleable by any environmental influences.

The nature of myths is to appear fixed and unchangeable. Yet if we understand how myths evolve and see how we participate in their creation, we can discern the possibility of transformation. In the actual process of editing myths, we are surprised to discover that what was once considered closed and permanently fossilized in our being is not only changeable but actually *awaiting* transformation.

Life Transitions and Crises Precipitate Transformation

Attribution, or assigning meaning to life experiences, is the result of our encounters with life transitions and traumatic events. Myths are formed from attributions that help us make sense of things. Life transitions and traumas such as accidents challenge our existing, attributed structure of meaning. Existing attributions are often inadequate in helping us respond to new challenges; they need to be modified to "explain" the new situational demands (Rediger, 1996). Failure to alter existing attributions in the face of new situational and transitional challenges hampers our ability to respond. Our emotional, interpersonal, and spiritual well-being is at stake.

Envisioning Our Role in Reauthoring Eases Transformation

Life will always present us with transitional and situational challenges. Existing attributions and myths need modifying, as a result. As we face challenges to our existing mythic formulations and interpretations of reality, not all of us will do the necessary editing and updating. Some of us resist changing them, feeling secure with what we already have done regarding our beliefs. Others of us, however, readily welcome the challenges and grow as a result. We see the new challenges as opportunities rather than dangers. What distinguishes those of us who envisage challenge as opportunity is what I call the "Columbus risk."

Christopher Columbus did not know with utter certainty that the world was not flat. He had to risk falling off the edge of the world in order to explore the future. The result was new discoveries—of a *preexistent* world, we should note. New attributions and myths about the nature of the world and the universe also resulted. Similarly, those of us willing to modify our existing myths need to be adventurous and risk-taking, as Columbus was. If we can risk going beyond what we can see with our own two eyes, we can bring about new horizons in our lives. Better self-understanding and new growth await us as we sail beyond our current horizons.

The Columbus risk comes with our understanding that part of our task is to modify the existing mythic structures that are informing (and limiting) our lives. In the reauthoring process, we must discern that our existing myths are alterable.

Re-storying Is Possible

Re-storying is possible when we discern new dimensions in our existing stories. Sometimes there is hidden meaning in existing stories; it remains obscure until we actually risk editing the existing attributions. White and Epston call these hidden possibilities "historical unique outcomes" (1990, p. 56). This refers to new possibilities that result when, in reediting our stories, we encounter new information from the past that contradicts the way information had been organized. Such discoveries can precipitate new meanings and attributions, which in turn assist in the re-storying process.

Transformation Means a New Perspective on Things

Change can come when we are able to reframe our experience. Reframing refers to putting experience into a different perspective, or framework, and thus envisioning new possibilities for life that were not initially evident. It can be said that reframing is not really change, because it shifts only the perspective and not the actual facts of the experience. Facts are interpreted so as to bring meaning to them; while there is merit in the argument that nothing has changed, nevertheless behavior generally follows changes in beliefs and convictions. Consequently, changing convictions and beliefs is a prerequisite for transforming behavior.

The Phases in Reauthoring Personal Myths

There are several stages in the reauthoring of personal myths:

1. Identify the themes that make up our personal myth.

2. Assess the influence of these themes on our lives over a period of time. This assessment determines if the themes are growth-facilitating or growth-inhibiting, and whether they contribute to our being wounded healers rather than remaining walking wounded.

3. Attempt to discern God's presence or a spiritual force at work in transforming these themes into themes of a wounded healer.

4. Make plans to alter the themes of the personal myth in order to increase our growth possibilities.

Establishing the Environment for Reauthoring

Prior to identifying the themes and subthemes of personal myths, we who seek to reauthor our myths must attend to several conditions conducive to successful reauthoring.

The most important one is to set a *proper environment or context* for the reauthoring process. The environmental context must be favorable to the reauthoring process: we need to give some attention to making sure that the atmosphere is safe, warm, and open. If we involve others in our reauthoring process, we must ensure that they are supportive and care about us. We must be sure that we discuss all expectations and goals. If we choose professional assistance, we need to do this based on the person's skills, training, and experience. We have to select a place for doing the reauthoring that is free from interruptions. We need to be relaxed and focused to get the most from the experience.

Creating a comfortable environment is essential, because reauthoring can be very threatening. Many of us have very debilitating and unhealthy myths at work in our lives. Changing these myths, although necessary, can provoke great anxiety because the existing myths and related behavior are known dimensions; they are predictable and bring a measure of security to our believing we know the future. Changing our beliefs and convictions threatens what is familiar and consistent. We will resist. We need to be aware of this reality and keep it in mind at all times.

Identifying Themes

You have already been given a series of questions designed to help you identify the themes in your personal mythologies. These questions, in the exercises at the end of Chapters Two, Three, and Four, are carefully designed to create an appropriately safe environment for your reauthoring process. I encourage you to use relaxation exercises if they will further your feeling of being at ease in this process. If you are undertaking the reauthoring process in a group, or with the direction of a leader, then another important aid in making the environment safe is self-disclosure by the leader. In self-disclosure, the leader shares aspects of her own early memories, birth myth, naming process, and other things that help bring participants on board in the process. As participants, we can envisage from the leader's self-disclosure how we might begin engaging in the reauthoring process ourselves; and of course disclosure helps reduce the anxiety of not knowing what to expect. It gives us some idea of what the process of reauthoring involves as well as insights and clues to what we need to do.

In my experience, most people are readily able to do the first exercise, exploring our earliest memories. Its purpose is to help us identify themes that are at work in our contemporary lives (Bagarozzi and Anderson, 1989). Generally, this opening exercise is nonthreatening; we usually identify only those themes we are emotionally ready to explore. Consequently, early memories are a good starting point for helping us identify the themes that make up our personal myth.

The second exercise, exploring our birth mythology, can be more anxiety-provoking for some people. Birth mythologies are the stories that significant others tell or told us about our conception, time in the womb, birth, and the first six months after birth (Rizzuto, 1979). They are significant because they deal with themes related to how we were welcomed into this world. I have seen people get up and leave the room when doing this part of the exercise. When I inquire, they indicate that the memories of what they found out about the circumstances of their birth are too painful; they don't want to feel the pain that comes with recollection. I try to warn people that there might be some pain in exploring birth mythologies. If it becomes too much for you, just stop the exercise. Don't feel obligated to finish it. Feel free to wait for a less-threatening exercise. In the reauthoring sessions that I conduct, I encourage people to approach me to discuss what it felt like to do the exercise. Most of them can then continue, and confront their feelings in small groups where they share what they felt in doing the exercise.

As we proceed through the other exercises related to personal myths, the themes unfold. We write them down; we are then ready to move to the next phase of the reauthoring process.

Mapping and Assessing

The second phase is mapping and assessing the impact of the personal myths on our lives. The myth we create is related to how we carry out our lives and live in our relationships. We begin tracing the themes of our personal myths: how they are associated with experiences we had early in our lives. We begin to correlate our current behavior with our interpretations of those early experiences. For example, one person traced a contemporary pattern in how she dealt with the men in her life to certain convictions she had come to regarding family-of-origin experiences; specifically, she felt that in order to be accepted she must always please those who had the potential to accept her. Other people seek a link between early-childhood assumption of responsibility and myths about their adult patterns and roles.

In assessing and mapping, we expect as an outcome that we will begin to envisage obstacles to our growth and happiness. These obstacles are caused by the myths that we created in response to the early experiences of our lives. We hope not only to visualize the problems encountered in our present functioning, but also to discover alternative ways to interpret the past as well as unique (but unnoticed) facts that might alter our present life scenarios (White and Epston, 1990). Often, current myths prevent us from discerning new meanings and different attributions. However, by identifying the myths at work in our lives in the present and mapping their influence, we find it easier to revise our notions of the past in light of new discoveries about it. Some reauthorers remember other events and experiences in their lives that challenge their original interpretation of the events, and they can then revise or reedit their long-standing beliefs and convictions.

I recall an example of a young African American adult. He was considering whether to answer a call to ministry but felt he could not because of his conviction that he had been deliberately abandoned by his mother. He felt that her deserting him had paralyzed his ability to care.

He had been raised by his grandparents but always wondered why his mother had not raised him. His conclusion was that he was not wanted. One day, he received the courage to sit down with his mother and explore why she had left him with his grandparents. She told him about the abusive relationship she was in after he was born, how she did not have the money for a refrigerator, and how she had to put his milk outside in the cold to keep it from spoiling. His mother confided that she had felt like an emotional wreck and for that reason thought her child would be better off with his grandparents. His mother's revelation was enough to help him revise his personal myth about being unwanted and abandoned.

The second stage in reauthoring helps us assess the impact of the myth on our lives. Sometimes the impact is both positive and negative. Mapping it gives those of us having negative myths the opportunity to begin revising them.

Discernment

The third stage of the reauthoring process is that of discerning the transforming forces at work, seeking to make the personal myths growth-facilitating. Identifying God's presence and work in our lives is a process unique to each of us. How we discern depends on a variety of things relating to how we carry out our spiritual discipline. Some of us use prayer to discern God's presence and help in our revising of our personal myths. An appropriate prayer of petition is to ask where God is working to bring healing to past relationships, and how God is helping us edit the beliefs and convictions we use to interpret life. Others turn to reading spiritual books, including the Bible. This approach focuses on discerning patterns of how God worked in the lives of biblical persons, in the belief that God continues to work in similar ways in the present and future. Some people identify with biblical characters, knowing that there are similarities in their own lives.

Or we may find God at work in our lives as we attempt to edit our personal myths, beginning with our work on the questionnaires that lead us to the themes of our personal myths. It may happen as we begin to review our call and its continued work in our lives. We may see God working through a slow process as we examine our lives in segments, in the different periods of time.

Just as we are able to map the influence of our personal myths on our lives, so too we are able to chart God's influence as challenges to the construction of our myths arise. Once we do this, we are ready to begin making plans.

Making Plans

The goal of reauthoring personal myths is to revise the story that runs through our personal behavior, to heal wounds and transform them into sources of strength in service to others. The identification, assessment, and discerning phases of the reauthoring process are all essential components to altering personal myths. Making plans is the final phase, wherein we outline the specific steps that will modify the myth.

The plans vary as widely as the individuals who make them. Some people contract with spiritual guides to explore in more depth their various mythologies. Some commit to doing research on their favorite biblical character, to learn more about how that person lived out his life. Some choose to enter personal counseling, while others seek accountability groups of peers to help them care for themselves better. Many choose the path of continuing education focused on spiritual disciplines. Some choose to be coached in how to go home, to work on family-of-origin issues.

Returning Home

This dimension of the reauthoring process is meant to gather information to fill in the gaps in our understanding of personal myths. Monica McGoldrick emphasizes that life patterns are multigenerational, and so it is important to trace the themes of the personal myths across several generations (McGoldrick, 1994).

Preston used a unique method to trace the legacy of his personal myth. He was interested in his own myth, but he also felt that knowing his father's personal myth might provide some clues into his own. He asked to interview his father, who agreed. Preston received a rare gift from reconnecting with his father in an extraordinary way. After the interview, Preston began writing up the results; he could clearly see the impact of previous generations on his life.

Preston took a great personal risk in approaching his father. He might have dredged up all the past hurts that he had felt at one time or another. He was at a point in his life, however, where he felt the risk was worth it, that he stood to gain more than he might lose. Although he approached his father fearfully, the result was that the pieces of his life fit together with new meaning.

Some people do not have the choice to return home. A woman approached me about a sermon I had just preached. She had spent many years in therapy working on her personal mythology, which centered around being sexually abused by her father. She had not been able to let go of her anger toward her father and hence had not revised her myth. But the sermon brought back a recollection: her father had approached her before he died and confessed his sin to her. She had not then been able to accept his confession, nor forgive him. In fact, she told me, she really did not believe he had actually admitted doing such a horrible thing. It was during the sermon, she said, that she fully recalled his confession of sorrow for his act. He had died several years earlier, but she said the Holy Spirit brought back his words so clearly that she could no longer distort what he said so as to go on protecting herself from pain. She was finally able to accept his apology from the past; she could forgive him. This breakthrough event enabled her to move on, to form a new myth for her life.

We can see that reauthoring personal myths has no specific timetable. It varies with each person, depending on the level of maturity, the severity of the problems involved, and other complex factors. Some people are able to revise their myths in a weekend retreat, while others may need much longer.

Reauthoring Marital and Family Myths

We can reauthor our marital myths as well, including both ideal-mate and ideal-marriage myths. This is true, too, with revising the family myths: ideal-child images and ideal-family images.

Revising marital and family myths follows the same phases as reediting personal myths. There comes a point in time where there must be a *symbolic* divorce and remarriage (to the same person) if the marriage is to grow and develop. There are times in marriage and family life when the old beliefs about men and women, children, marriage, and family life must be changed to meet the realities that people are facing. Such times of change may be moments in which individuals, marriages, and families face life-cycle transitions; when they face threats from outside the marriage and family, such as discrimination, unemployment, economic hardship, dislocation, and others; and when the myths that govern marital and family life are no longer adequate to meet the needs of those involved. When myths are no longer adequate, the family has an opportunity to change the myths, for the individuals, the marriage, and the family.

Change in marriage and family life can be "first order" or "second order" change (Nichols and Everett, 1986, p. 130). First-order change is returning the marriage or family system to the original dynamic state that existed prior to the impetus for change. In this form of change, the marital and family myths remain intact. Second-order change refers to actually reauthoring (editing) the marital and family myths so that the original myths are altered considerably and the behavior of those involved is substantially affected. In some cases, marriages and families experience both first-order and second-order changes, depending on what the precipitating events are.

Editing marital myths means altering ideal images of our mate and what our marriage should be. I often do pastoral counseling with people whose lives are disrupted because one or both spouses are in seminary. Seminary is often a triggering factor in facing marital partners with the need to revise or reedit personal myths. Most often, changing the marital myth begins with identifying the marital difficulty and the family-of-origin patterns that influence the problem. We explore ideal-mate and ideal-marriage images as part of the family-of-origin influences.

Depending on the level of pain in the marriage and the level of reactivity between the spouses, this identification step can take one session or as many as are needed for the spouses to recognize the sources of their ideal images. Reactivity stems from our emotional attachment to our own family of origin and the degree to which we feel we must resist changing that attachment (Guerin, Fay, Burden, and Kautto, 1987). Spouses who have a good measure of self-distinction from the family of origin can explore the source of the ideal-mate images in the family of origin with some dispatch. Those who are more attached have more difficulty. In the latter case, many counseling sessions might be needed before moving to the next phase of the reauthoring process.

The seminary experience often triggers marital and family difficulties for students. There are two quite common causes: the student has to commit emotional energy to the seminary experience, or the curriculum work precipitates his or her personal growth. In the first instance, the seminary experience challenges the student's assumptions about life and how life should be lived in light of faith. This is often a traumatic experience, and the student often withdraws emotional energy from marriage and family relationships in order to invest it in dealing with the challenges to her or his way of viewing life and faith. When this withdrawing and reinvesting is taking place, the marital partner and children know immediately. Feelings of being abandoned often result along with marital stress. In the second instance, the pace of personal growth accelerates because of new and intense experiences that the student undergoes with peers, in the classroom, and in supervised ministerial encounters. These experiences also upset the seminary student's marital and family stability. They exert severe pressure on marriage and family, and marital adjustment is often necessary. For some, a marital crisis results, and intervention is needed.

I have found that couples with good enough separation from their families of origin can respond to a retreat model of reediting. They are often emotionally free from the roles and dynamics that they endured in the family of origin such that they can invest that energy in the reauthoring. They have the requisite ego-strength to identify ideal-mate and ideal-marriage themes, map the influence such themes have on their marriage, discern God's work in helping them change, and make plans to follow through on the changes once they leave the retreat. I have also found, however, that persons with less-than-optimal separation from family-of-origin roles and dynamics need marital counseling or personal counseling before they can begin to approach the reauthoring process. That is, some persons don't have the necessary emotional freedom or energy to devote to their own growth. They need to become a self in the family of origin before they can commit themselves to the work of reauthoring.

Distinguishing oneself from family-of-origin roles and dynamics is known as self-differentiation; it is vital to reediting our marital and family myths. People with relatively good self-distinction can engage in the reauthoring process of their ideal-child, ideal-parent, and ideal-family myths in a retreat format. Others with less self-distinction need marital and family counseling.

The Singletons and Houstons, whom we met in Chapter Three, are examples of parents who had clear ideal-child expectations. In both cases, they had to alter the expectations for each child to some extent, differently depending on the child and the family's circumstances. Moreover, each of these four parents had an ideal-parenting expectation for himself and herself that also became part of the family mythology.

Their reauthoring process followed the same process we have already identified. Each parent had to examine his or her ideal images of child and parenting. Each also had to assess whether such images helped him or her deal with the real child and the real situation. In the case of the Singletons, Mitchell had good self-differentiation and was willing to alter his ideal expectations, or at least suspend them. Nicky, however, was tied too closely to the parenting expectations of her family of origin and lacked the necessary self-differentiation to begin the reauthoring process. Consequently, she could not change her ideal-child expectations or deal with the fact that she might not be the ideal parent. This produced too much anxiety for her; she undertook family counseling but withdrew. She also withdrew emotionally from her son Clarence as a result. Mitchell and Clarence continued family counseling, and the father took on all the responsibility for dealing with his son as he (the father) proceeded to modify his ideal-child expectations.

The Houstons were very different. Each of the parents had good self-differentiation. When they assessed their own ideal-parenting expectations, they discovered that the images were not working. Their expectations regarding Brittany's maturity were not consistent with her age, and as parents they were not responding to their child's real needs. This embarrassed them, temporarily. But they had the necessary ego-strength to admit their mistakes, and they began to alter their style of relating to Brittany to correspond to her developmental needs.

Both the Singletons and the Houstons were part of my counseling load. The counseling with the Singletons took many sessions, mainly because of Nicky's low level of self-differentiation. In the case of the Houstons, however, the intervention was very brief—three sessions, in fact. This was because each parent had a high level of self-differentiation. The lower the level of self-differentiation, the more threatening is the reauthoring process. The reverse is also true, with greater self-differentiation being less of a threat.

Both the Singletons and the Houstons were religious; both fathers were religious caregivers. Both felt that creating an environment for the growth and development of each child was important in the sight of God. Therefore, it was important to them how they lived as family members and raised their children. Annette Houston also felt the same way. Nicky Singleton, however, was angry that God had given her such a recalcitrant son and wondered why he could not have been more like her daughter, Grace, who fully met her ideal.

Let us not view Nicky as the bad apple here. In fact, she epitomizes what the experience of reauthoring is often like. For most people, the process raises anxiety because change can disrupt secure ways of thinking and behaving. It is safe, and prudent, to expect moments of anger and pain during the process—moments when it would be more comfortable to stop.

Reauthoring Ministerial Mythologies

Identifying ministerial myths, assessing or mapping their influence on the caregiver's life, discerning God's presence in the work to alter the myths, and making plans to change them are the phases in reauthoring ministerial myths as well. Here, I want to focus primarily on phase three: the role of the call (whether ongoing or subsequent to beginning this work) in the process of reediting ministerial myths. The emphasis here is on discerning God's presence in the reauthoring process.

God's Presence

In Chapter One, I suggested that the etiology of spiritual renewal is in recalling our original motivation for ministry. I described my father's rehearsing his call as an example of a traditional model for spiritual renewal. In that introductory model, I said very little about my understanding of the period of liminality, the "in-between time" (following the original call) that leads to a subsequent call or renewal. The period of liminality is one in which our call is renewed daily; because it is often during a retreat, the liminal time deepens our call and our commitment to religious vocation. Liminality or in-between time is when new models or visions of reality are disclosed; it is when we begin to envision or imagine new possibilities for our lives. The subsequent call, as a moment of liminality, renews, reignites, and reawakens old passions and directions for ministry. The in-between time period continues to remove old blocks to our meaningful commitment to ministry; it continues to reauthor and revitalize lesser myths. It puts God's imagination in our heads, and new possibilities for our ministry surface.

The subsequent call of God at moments of liminality is a work of God, as was the original call. Because the call is ongoing, it is possible to discern God's presence again as we find our call renewed in moments of liminality.

A Personal Story of Reauthoring

Permit me to narrate my own renewing and updating of my ministerial mythology, that is, my own experience with a second call in a moment of liminality. In February 1992 I began to be aware of chest pain about eight minutes into my regular jogging routine. I also discovered that the pain abated when I stopped exercising. When I first felt the pain, I went to my primary physician, who then sent me to a cardiologist. The cardiologist gave me a stress test and a treadmill examination to check my heart. The stress test registered normal; I experienced no pain when doing the examination, and the cardiologist pronounced me fit from a cardiovascular point of view.

I continued to have chest pain when exercising, however. My primary physician sent me back to the same cardiologist who told me that, in his experience as a heart specialist, my treadmill results meant that I had no heart problems. He then attributed my problems to exercise-induced asthma. I spent several months getting checked out for this new diagnosis. When asthma was ruled out, the doctors settled on esophagal reflux, since the pain was in the esophagus area of my chest. The pain persisted, and in early December 1994 I changed primary physicians. I was immediately diagnosed as having angina. During testing, I went into heart distress during heart catheterization and had to have immediate surgery. On December 8, I had quadruple bypass surgery—after two years of complaining about chest pain. During bypass surgery, the doctors discovered that my left main artery was more than 99 percent closed. The medical people said they couldn't understand why I had not had a massive heart attack. They said this kind of artery disease was a "widow maker." While some physicians marveled at my good fortune, other physicians attributed my miraculous survival to God.

This miracle of surviving arterial disease without any heart damage at all was only the physical side of my story. There is another. It is about renewal and the reauthoring of my ministerial mythology.

During the two-year period of failed diagnosis, I was depressed. I was depressed about my failing physical health because of my inability to exercise, and I was also worried about what to do for my aging parents, who had reached the point where they were unable to care for themselves any longer. They were resisting all efforts by others to help or intervene in their lives, and I didn't know what to do. My wife noticed that I really seemed no longer to care if I lived or died. It was at that point that we decided to find a way for my parents to come to live with us. (They have now been living with us since December 1993.) My parents' coming to live with us released me from one aspect of my depression considerably.

After my surgery, and during my recovery period in the hospital, I had a moment of liminality. The still, small voice of God came to me almost inaudibly. Suddenly, a question came to my mind. It was clear. It was, "Do you accept what I have done for you?" My mental response was, "What do you mean?" But what I said in response was, "Of course." Then the thought came to me: accepting God's miracle in my life means accepting a new purpose and focus for my life. I believe the voice was trying to tell me that my work on earth is not done; God intervened to make sure that I stay around to complete the work that has been given to me. At that moment, I realized that the remaining years of my life are to be driven by a deeper sense of calling and purpose than I had prior to my surgery.

The reauthoring of my ministerial mythology has a key element: reaffirmation that I cannot do ministry as a loner any longer. My personal mythology, marital mythology, and ministry mythology all rested on the theme of being a loner. It has become clear to me that my ministry is God's ministry, not "mine," and that God has become a companion to me and provided me with others to be in partnership with me as I carry out ministerial tasks. I have a renewed sense of God's intent for me and God's presence at work in my life. I know that I was given new life by God for a particular purpose. I was given a second chance to live my life differently.

Since my surgery and spiritual moment of liminality, I have become a vegetarian and begun to live in ways that take better care of my whole self. I have a better balance between work, recreation, spirituality, and nurturing relationships. I seek more mutual relationships than I once did. I tend not to overfunction, as I once did. I no longer see ministry and my life as a pilgrimage isolated from other people.

At the time of writing, it has been two years since my heart surgery. The major impact of the surgery on my ministry seems to be in the way people now respond to me. I seem to be regarded as one of the elders who are in charge of the faith traditions that must be preserved and passed on to the next generations. I turned fifty just prior to the surgery; at that time I saw myself as a disciple, still learning the traditions of caring and of faith. I did not consciously see myself as one of the elders, as a steward or guardian of the mysteries of the faith. However, following my surgery, it has become very clear to me that I was promoted: from the ranks of a disciple to the ranks of a steward.

From a developmental point of view, moving from disciple to steward means that I have reoriented my life from being based on external societal standards to a more inner and spiritual orientation (Jung, 1933). Wisdom has taken center stage, and I seem to be less driven by meeting external standards of success. I am not as intimidated as I once was by meeting expectations of perfection. I seem to be living more on grace and less by the demands or expectations of others. I seem to be more at peace with myself and happy with what I have done and am currently doing. I can accept what I have and that I have not achieved better. I am more comfortable with my spontaneous life in that I can express more of my feelings, and I can tolerate intimacy better. I seem to be more emotionally available to others than prior to my surgery. Finally, I think I am more in touch with the unfolding of God's story in my life, and I can allow myself to better cooperate with what God is doing in my life. In the words of my therapist, I am learning to love and be loved.

Spiritual renewal of caregivers rests on renewal of our original call. The original call is renewed by a subsequent call or calls, which take place at key moments of our lives. These key moments are not unlike those original moments when we were sure God was calling us. The subsequent calls can come at any time and at any point in our lives. They can come during spiritual retreats, spiritual guidance, pastoral counseling, or ordinary moments of our everyday existence. At these times, our lives suddenly come into clear focus, and a new awareness dawns on us.

Summary

The reediting process involves (1) identifying the themes at work in the various mythologies in our lives, (2) mapping or charting the influence that these themes have had on us and our ministry, (3) discerning where God's renewing influence is as we come to grips with these themes and their influences, and (4) making plans that will aid us in changing some of the themes. As we mature toward knowing ourselves apart from our family-of-origin patterns, we can enter the reauthoring process with relative ease and profit more from reauthoring. Those of us less able to distinguish ourselves from our family of origin, however, have difficulty reauthoring our myths. We need a therapeutic environment, and ongoing spiritual direction, where we can work through our resistance and anxiety about change.

6

SUZANNE

ALLOWING THE TRUE SELF TO SURFACE

HIDING ONE'S GIFTS in order to please others and be feminine is a major strategy that some women use to make the transition from adolescence into adulthood. Under pressure from family-of-origin expectations, roles, and dynamics, as well as cultural gender notions, many young adult women have learned to hide their true selves and identities. This can be particularly devastating for ministry as well as to the sense of identity of the religious caregiver.

This chapter is about a religious caregiver, whom I call Suzanne, and how she developed a personal mythology based on her feelings of rejection and hiding her gifts and talents. It describes how she moved from being unaware of her personal myth, and the influence that the myth had on her life and ministry, to awareness and the start of reauthoring her personal myth to benefit self-formation and her ministry. Suzanne's story shows how hiding one's true self in order to please others hampers ministry and why it is important to revise personal myths that hinder our effectiveness.

Suzanne

Suzanne is a single African American in her mid-twenties. She is a senior in seminary and struggling to develop her confidence in her ministerial gifts. Taking off a year from seminary to do an internship in ministry, she hopes to learn to claim her gifts for ministry and demonstrate them without hesitation or apology. As a member of a mainline, predominantly white denomination, she knows she needs to be less bashful in claiming her gifts and allowing her light to shine more.

89

Suzanne faces a major problem: her reluctance to assume leadership roles in ministry. While her calling to ministry is clear to her, there is something holding her back from exercising her gifts and leadership ability in ministerial roles. She comes across as preferring to remain in the background, keeping her light hidden from others. At times she appears to be an adolescent, just trying to get along and not ruffle too many feathers. She is the epitome of the good girl. She likes being liked, and if assuming leadership roles means she might not be liked, she will hesitate in taking those roles.

In a year-long group therapy class prior to her senior year in seminary, she received feedback from her peers concerning her gifts, especially her people skills. She was told that she was very approachable and likeable and that people liked being around her. She was also very intelligent and had much insight into things that she kept to herself most of the time. Her peers also delineated her growing edge: her reluctance to assume her uniqueness on the basis of her gifts. It appeared to them that she would rather be one of the group than stand out. Realizing that these comments were accurate and could have a negative impact on her future ministry, she decided to explore why she behaved the way she did.

I gladly steered Suzanne toward the model of reauthoring her personal mythology, believing that part of the problem she was facing related to convictions about herself. She began the reauthoring process because she was motivated by a desire to be more effective in ministry; learning to share her gifts and talents was one way to do so.

Suzanne points out that the dominant theme running through her personal myth is her relationship with her mother. She was the youngest child and had many rebellious ideas; therefore she was labeled the black sheep by her mother. While birth-order studies would explain her behavior in that light, her mother's constant remarking on her rebellious behavior left Suzanne permanently scarred. In truth, she felt rejected in believing she was a rebel; the seeds were sown for her to suppress that side of herself later in adolescence to win her mother's favor.

Her mother would also regularly accuse her pejoratively of resembling her father's side of the family. Suzanne viewed this too as a loss, as further rejection by her mother. Her parents were divorced, and her mother had many unresolved issues with regard to her former husband. Whenever Suzanne's mother was displeased with her, she would say, "You're definitely your father's child." Because of such negative attributions about her behavior, Suzanne felt alienated from her mother and alone in the world. She felt rejected as well as misunderstood.

Suzanne indicates that her mother's attitude toward her resulted in a great need to try to meet her mother's expectations. She tried to please her mother, but nothing she did seemed to make a positive difference. She also believed she had to work very hard to overcome the childhood badge of dishonor of resembling her father's side of the family. Hence at some point in her early life, she decided to hide her true self, thinking this would please her mother.

At the point of Suzanne's exploration of the major themes in her personal myth, she revealed that her mother's attitude has affected her relationships with men. She is not sure of the connection between her mother's attitude and her behavior, but she believes that she is attracted to men who are like her father.

The rejection that Suzanne feels began when she was caught up in the marital difficulties and pain of her parents. The dominant themes of her personal myth took shape. She believed she was expected to be the savior of her parents' relationship; but as a result, she was pulled in two different directions. Her mother suspected she was more supportive of her father, which added to her feeling of alienation. In turn, her mother said that Suzanne had deserted her for her father, and so Suzanne felt she had lost her mother's love as a consequence. From this loss of relationship with her mother, Suzanne formulated her goal in life of winning her mother's favor. But that primary motivation, to do things that would win her mother's approval, never seemed to result in returned love. Unrequited love became another important theme for Suzanne. It fed the myth of rejection, because she concluded that if she were different, she would be loved.

Suzanne's desire to win her mother's love became one of the commanding forces shaping her own view of who she is as well as how she relates to the world. She has always been recovering from multiple love losses, beginning with loss of her father's love as a consequence of the divorce. Suzanne decided not to connect with her father after the divorce, for fear that that would further alienate her mother.

Because of the several losses of significant others in her life, Suzanne has suffered significant emotional wounds. She says she is always seeking salvation. She looks for people to replace her parents or replace the void left by her parents.

Given the major themes of rejection and loss in Suzanne's personal myth, it is important to explore the different dimensions of her personal myth to envision how other themes have combined with the dominant theme of rejection to shape her life.

Identifying Suzanne's Themes

The Earliest Memory

In response to one item on the questionnaire, regarding her personal myth, Suzanne realized that her earliest memories relate to themes she is currently dealing with. She believes her early memory of hugging was an attempt to hold on to her mother and get her mother to return affection:

> My earliest memory that I have in my family of origin was lying and sitting in my mother's lap in church and at home. Sleeping with my mother, anxiously waiting for her to come to bed, yelling, "Ma, you coming?" Finally, playing at home with my cousin while other siblings were away in school, I found my father in bed with another woman.
>
> I was always very comforted by my mother. I stuck very close to her. I imagine this came as a result of being the youngest. I believe this is the earliest memory that I have. I see this theme still present today. That is, my mother often tells me to stop hugging her so much. I felt close to her and I also felt close to my father. At the time I saw him with this woman in bed, I did not understand exactly what was taking place. As I got older, I realized that my father betrayed my mother.
>
> I realize now that the hugging and the affection I showed my mother and the betrayal of my mother by my father are related to themes that are present in my life today. I see myself seeking out parental figures in my life, and my hugging them is a way to win their favor.

She also realizes that her father's infidelity contributed to her eventually losing his love and affection. Ultimately, it was the marital difficulty between her father and mother that made youthful life miserable for her. This marital pain made it difficult for Suzanne to connect with either parent. Her mother expected her to feel the way she felt about Suzanne's father, and this left her feeling ambivalent toward him.

There is still a void in Suzanne's life. She has not found Mr. Right. All of the men in her life seem to resemble her father; specifically, they have the same inclination to womanizing. She does not want to lead the same kind of miserable marital life that her mother had. Even in associating with mentors in her ministry, she attaches herself to those who are like parental figures. She has been fortunate to find some mentors who recognize and nurture her gifts of ministry.

Birth Mythology

Suzanne believes that her mother felt the timing of her conception and birth was bad. Her parents were having grave marital difficulties, and her mother did not want to conceive then. This sense of being rejected by her mother continues in the present because her mother has been unable to accept her decision to be a minister.

Suzanne's father, she has learned from relatives, was excited about her birth. He was proud to have a daughter.

God plays an important role in her birth story. Exploring her birth myth, she says she learned to depend on God and God's acceptance of her. With so much rejection in her family of origin, her God image has much to do with the degree to which she feels welcomed in this world. Whereas she feels let down by her parents, she feels lifted up by the presence of God in her life. She says she has felt God's presence in her life from a very early age.

Birth Order

There were nine children connected with Suzanne's parents. Her father had five children from a previous marriage, and her mother had one child prior to marrying Suzanne's father. There were three children born of that marriage; Suzanne is the youngest.

In many ways, Suzanne's behavior is consistent with that of the classic youngest child. She went her own way and has developed her life in ways other family members have not. She chose ministry as a profession, differently from any family member. In some ways she was and is a rebel; her mother often reacted to her as such. Despite her mother's warnings not to have much to do with her father, she rebelled at times and sought him out for a relationship.

Gender and Sex

Suzanne speculates that her mother must have been happy that she had a girl. She reasons that if she had been a boy, her mother would have been even more rejecting of her, by identifying the child with his father.

Names and Nicknames

With regard to names and nicknames, Suzanne says that her mother did not name her; a friend of her mother's did. What makes matters worse in Suzanne's mind is that the name came from a TV show the friend had been watching at the moment she was asked. Suzanne has remained offended by her parents' not thinking enough of her to have chosen a name themselves.

Her mother did give her a nickname: Suzanne was the "Mason baby." This was her father's family name. That fact intensified Suzanne's childhood feelings of rejection, because she knew the negative connotations that Mason had for her mother.

Peer and Sibling Relationships

Peer and sibling relationships have helped to prepare the ground for her ministry. It was her mother who labeled her the black sheep in the family. However, as Suzanne grew older, her brothers and sisters became aware of her special interests and gifts and came to her for spiritual guidance and religious perspectives. They looked up to her and gave her a leadership role in their lives regarding these concerns.

She says her role as religious confidante for her brothers and sisters came with a price. Having always sensed she was different, she felt even more like a misfit with them. They had different standards, values, and religious outlooks, although they respected her religious insight. "I never really engaged in girl talk or talk about sex, and they accepted me in this role," she says.

Roles

Suzanne played two different roles in her family. With regard to her mother, she was the black sheep. With her brothers and sisters, she played a religious role. Their acceptance of her in the religious role helped her feel wanted to some extent; it helped her deal with the rejection she felt with her mother and father.

Parental Discipline

As for parental discipline, Suzanne believes she was punished more than her brothers and sisters. She resigned herself to such treatment, reasoning that she might as well do what she wished since she was going to get disciplined whether she deserved it or not. About punishment, she says, "It made me bitter; I felt that my mother did not like me."

Discipline in school was similar to what she received at home. She showed a bad attitude and teachers did not put up with it. Once she was suspended from school. She has some guilt over her youthful rebellious attitude, and she deduces that maybe she deserved disciplined treatment because of her poor attitude. She is only now connecting her misbehavior with her feelings of being rejected.

Story Identification

Suzanne's story identification relates more to her role with her brothers and sisters, but it laid the ground for her ministry:

> My favorite fairy tale is the "Mother Hen," who was cooking and could not find anyone to help her cook. When it came time to eat, everyone wanted to come and eat. My favorite character is the mother hen, because she was able to handle the situation alone. Throughout the story, she was asking for help and busily doing all of the work. At the end, I believe, she fed everyone and told them of how they needed to correct their selfish behavior. The characters I dislike the most are all of the baby hens and other characters, because they all made excuses not to help. Throughout the story, they sat on their behinds and did nothing. At the end, the mother hen told them the lesson of the need to give and not just receive, and she fed them.

This story identification affirms a major effort that Suzanne made to please her mother. Taking over the mothering role for her brothers and sisters, she hoped she would receive acceptance for doing this. But her mother was never pleased. Suzanne says her mother has still not really accepted her in the ministerial role. Suzanne continues to feel that the theme of rejection dominates her life.

Mapping and Assessing

Suzanne's dominant theme of rejection relates to her mother's conviction that she favored, and resembled, her father's side of the family. As a result of this belief, Suzanne has spent most of her life trying to please her mother and win her affection. She also believes that her attraction to the wrong kind of men relates to her father and the pattern he established with her mother. She is attracted to men who will not be faithful to her, and this of course fuels her sense of rejection. Suzanne has identified with her mother and how her father mistreated her mother. This identification often happens with the same-sex offspring when there is spousal misconduct. She has come to believe that mistreatment is all she can expect in life.

Suzanne also believes she is still caught in the triangular relationship with her mother and her father. In triangulation, a third party is drawn into a troubled marital relationship in order to lessen the pain and conflict (Nichols, 1984). Suzanne wanted desperately to have a father-daughter relationship, but she did not pursue it aggressively for fear of losing her mother. As a result, her pursuit of her own self-interests and personal goals was and has been reluctant. Her stronger motivation remains to fulfill what others expect of her. At times, however, she still rebels and is uncooperative. This rebellion is self-destructive and self-defeating, of course; she feels it has affected her academic performance throughout her life. She sees herself as the classic underachiever, who has not really developed her true self or her true abilities. The positive side of her rebelliousness is that it helps her identify her true self (even if she fails to carry through on that development); she does feel the need to bring into better harmony her rebellious self and her approval-seeking self. The real self, she senses, lies somewhere between these two extremes.

At first, she was reluctant to map the influence of the theme of rejection on her ministry. She resisted because it could mean facing real change. Finally, she gave up as she discovered that her reluctance to let her light shine in ministry related so strongly to her family-of-origin dynamics. She understands that not being affirmed by her mother in her ministry contributes greatly to lack of confidence in her own ministerial gifts. Although her sisters and brothers recognized and affirmed those gifts, throughout her younger life it was as if the gifts did not exist just because her mother failed to acknowledge them.

These observations have come as Suzanne traces the influence of the dominant themes of her personal myth on her life. In pursuing the impact of these themes, she sets the stage for altering the hold that her personal myth has over her life. She believes that having been triangulated and rejected contributed to a growth-inhibiting personal myth that has locked her into negative patterns of behavior. She recognizes the need to alter her personal myth.

Discernment

The third stage of the reauthoring process is discerning the transforming forces at work, to seek a more growth-facilitating personal myth.

Suzanne has had a sense of God's presence in her life since she was a small child. She felt the presence with her as she walked through the house as a little girl. She used to tell her mother, "I feel God following me, and every time I turn around to see him, he's not there." Because God was present in her childhood, she believes God is present now as she attempts to rewrite the dominant themes that make up her personal myth.

One way in which she has sought discernment is through prayer. She sees that God is working in her, trying to help her heal her relationship with her mother. From this revelation, she has found encouragement to begin doing work that may eventually help that relationship.

In seeking to renew her relationship with her mother, she finds that reading books helps her understand how God is guiding her through the journey of renewal of broken relationships. She sees God at work in her life helping her release harmful memories. She feels she has an unforgiving spirit and holds onto the hurt and pain of those who hurt her. God is leading her to see that she only hurts herself and prevents her own growth by not letting go of things from the past. She feels she has to learn to let go if she is to mature and have an effective ministry.

She is learning how holding on to painful memories is self-destructive. She is giving the hurt feelings over to God for healing. She finds that God is helping her understand the true meaning of forgiveness, and she sees how her life improves when she does not hold onto past hurts.

Making Plans

The goals in reauthoring our personal myths are to revise the story that determines personal behavior, to heal wounds, and to transform them into service to others. The identification, assessment, and discerning phases of the reauthoring process are all essential components to altering the personal myth. Making plans is the final phase, where we outline specific steps for future modification of the personal myth.

Suzanne has outlined her planned steps for reauthoring: (1) to seek spiritual and professional guidance beyond seminary, to explore further the themes in her personal myth, (2) to explore how the themes perpetuate themselves in her behavior, and (3) to allow God's presence to heal the hurts and wounds that continue to influence her life.

Cultural Factors

Suzanne traces her feelings of rejection to her mother's indifference to her gifts and interests, and to the fallout of her parents' marital conflict. Rejection is clearly rooted in how Suzanne has interpreted and attributed significance to her parents' behavior. Her own loyalty to both mother and father left her caught, because her mother believed Suzanne's commitment was more to her father and so her mother withdrew affection from her.

Suzanne could have responded in any number of ways to perceiving rejection. She could have protested, ignoring her mother's expectations and becoming the very opposite of a model daughter. Rather, she chose to become a "conforming angel," who tries to please her mother in every way, even denying her gifts and graces. The decision to hide her talents under a bush (to use a biblical metaphor), thinking this would win back her mother's love, contributed greatly to the development of her negative personal mythology.

The strategy of hiding our talent brings to mind the cultural strategy girls use in making the transition from childhood to adolescence. When the girl experiences tension between her inner needs and what is deemed good and valuable under the influence of cultural messages, she may seek to dissociate from those inner qualities that are regarded as undesirable (Taylor, Gilligan, and Sullivan, 1995). With this maneuver, the girl loses touch with her own voice and her inner sense of vitality and strength.

What is significant about the dissociation strategy in dealing with dissonance between self-perception and the perception of others is that it is culturally sanctioned. Suzanne's choice was not idiosyncratic; this hiding strategy is long-standing and culturally blessed. Cultural and family-of-origin dynamics combined to shape Suzanne's interpretation of reality and her responses to what she experienced.

Important Changes for Suzanne

Suzanne's response to her feelings of rejection, namely, to hide her talents, was a self-destructive move. The biblical metaphor of burying talents points to the reality that buried talents leads to human atrophy (Matthew 25: 14--30 and Luke 19: 12–27). Suzanne's approach to winning her mother's love was a way of sabotaging her self-development. To grow and become an effective person and minister, she needs to make some changes in her personal mythology. Her peers sense that her hiding tactic makes her ineffective in the ministry she wants to pursue. How can she change?

Suzanne came to seminary unaware that there was anything amiss with hiding her true self. However, when she enrolled in the group therapy course for a year, she began a slow process of coming to awareness of her hiding pattern. Her peers and the teacher enabled her to get a first glimpse of the pattern. The course was in the second year of her seminary pilgrimage; she then took a one-year internship to work on reclaiming her true self while engaging in ministry. After that, she returned to seminary to complete her senior year.

In the first semester back from her intern year, she registered in a course I entitled "Pastoral Care and Inner Healing." The course was intended to enable students to use the model of reauthoring presented in this book. Suzanne was ready to look systematically at her personal mythology; she brought to the course some awareness that she had gifts of insight and caring that she often hid. Wanting to explore why she chose to hide these gifts, she used the course to formally engage in the reauthoring process. The results of her work are evident in this chapter.

Suzanne's reauthoring was truly a "process"; it took place over nearly two and a half years. She was not alone in the process; she had significant companionship from her peers, supervisors, and teachers. Gradually, she was able to replace the internalized, intimidating expectations (from both her mother and from the larger culture) that had led her to hide her talents. She used the available support to risk being herself.

The expectations of others are often internalized and become a set of unrealistic standards calling for sacrifice of self. Merle Jordan deems this internalization of unrealistic demands religious idolatry. Idolatry is the elevation of a secondary value to primary status in our life, to the extent that this elevated figure becomes the primary means of self-evaluation (Jordan, 1985). When this happens, we give over the self to a tyranny of expectations that destroy it. To overcome this tyranny, we must replace the internalized expectations with a more accepting and realistic expectation. That comes from caring others, who are committed to helping us realize our true self.

Suzanne found these others in her peers, supervisors, and teachers. They were all committed to her growth and development, and they made themselves available for her to carry out her positive internalization. When she internalized others (peers, supervisors, and teachers), they became an enduring source of nurturing expectations that sustained her as she slowly allowed her true self to emerge from hiding.

Suzanne's story teaches us that changing a personal myth takes time. It is aided by being in relationship with significant others who care. Without such caring relationships, the reauthoring process is almost impossible.

What Suzanne Found Helpful in Others

Suzanne found help from others as she engaged in the reauthoring process. They told their stories after she told hers. They listened to her stories. They showed interest in her welfare. They were willing to gently challenge her when she hid her experience. They were patient with her as her true self slowly emerged. Suzanne's peers, supervisors, and teachers were willing to share their own experiences, and she found that their sharing facilitated her growth. She understood these persons were genuinely committed to her growth. Their interest in her, their willingness to consistently confront her hiding, and their acceptance of her own pacing in the self-realization process were all essential help in her reauthoring process as well.

The Role of Reconnecting with the Call

Suzanne's call has been a continuing factor in her reauthoring process. Reconnecting with it has helped her make a decision not to bury her gifts. The reconnection gives her permission to claim her gifts and to render her mother's expectations of her secondary. Getting back in touch with her call has helped her to discern the priorities for her life and ministry:

> Deep down inside, I always had a desire to share the Gospel. As a youth, I sat down and thought about the most effective ways to do it. I noticed that the company that I kept was always with women in ministry, and I would continuously be concerned with how they carried out their ministries and wondered when they knew they were called. Soon after, I began to realize that God was also calling me to the preaching ministry.
>
> My call is a major motivating factor in my life today. As I endeavor to use my gifts for ministry, I feel my call is the only thing that has sustained me as I seek to make the changes I need to make in order to be effective.

Suzanne's call reminds her that ministry is her vocational choice and that her growth as a person and as a professional depends on developing her God-given gifts. The remembrance of the call helps sustain her and give her courage to take the necessary risks she must make to reauthor her personal myth.

Conclusion

Suzanne brought to seminary a personal myth of rejection that caused her to hide her talents for ministry. It was hindering her ability to be effective in relationships and ministry. With the aid of peers, teachers, and supervisors, she was able to enter and carry out the reauthoring process successfully. Her deep feeling of rejection led to self-rejection, but reauthoring her personal myth allowed her to reclaim her true self and a willingness to manifest that self in ministry. The process has been a long one, but immensely meaningful for her.

7

JAMES AND HOPE

UNDERSTANDING WHO CALLED US TO MINISTRY

THERE IS A STRONG and valued religious tradition in the United States concerning calling and vocation. The understanding of a call is strongly associated with biblical tradition (Achtemeier, 1985; *Interpreter's Dictionary of the Bible*, 1993; and Richardson and Bowden, 1983). The biblical understanding of the call refers to divine election or commission to take our place in God's salvation plan. This call is particular to religious specialists as well as for religious people in general. As it survives in the United States, this understanding of the call is still something initiated by God, drawing persons into a special service to God and to humanity.

The two cases presented in this chapter reflect very traditionally the biblical sense of the call. In fact, Hope, a Euro-American, and James, who is African American, belong to denominations where individuals are expected to have a clear sense of having been called, and clarity about what one's call is.

The cases presented here are significant because these two persons are very clear about their call to ministry. However, questions emerge for them whether the call they received has come clearly from God or from their families of origin. There is a second concern: are the call and the related roles imposed on them irrespective of who they really are, or are the roles they play in ministry consistent with their own self-understanding and gifts?

Examining personal myths has helped these two people clarify for themselves that the call came from both God and the members of their families of origin. Moreover, they have also gained some measure of freedom to choose the roles they play in ministry, thanks to exploration of their personal myths.

It is important to clarify family-of-origin issues and their impact on our call because the demands of ministry eventually force us to clarify our reasons for being in ministry. Thus, if we use ministry to work through family-of-origin issues, we eventually hit a dead end; we then have to decide whether our reasons for being in ministry are related to God. Being in ministry primarily to work through family-of-origin issues makes it difficult to handle those dark nights of the soul with which ministry is concerned. However, if we truly feel our call is from God, we can separate out our family-of-origin concerns and find ways to remain faithful to what God has called us to do. To enter the struggles of ministry fueled only by family-of-origin concerns jeopardizes our ministry and our emotional well-being.

James: The Myth of Sole Responsibility

James is a single African American in his late twenties. When he came to retreat, he had served several churches as pastor for about five years and was interested in exploring his call to the ministry in a safe setting. His motivation for attending the ministerial retreat was that he did not seem as enthusiastic about ministry as he had earlier. He wanted to find out why.

He had some seminary training but was unable to complete it. He belongs to a nonconnectional denomination that takes the autonomy of the local congregation very seriously. He is the son of a preacher and was raised to respect the tradition of the "religious call." He understands the call as something God does; he believes we have no choice whether to accept the call or not. For him, to refuse to accept the call is tantamount to committing suicide. He believes that once called, our destiny has a clear direction. To refuse this destiny, he believes, is to cut ourselves off from the major source of life.

James struggles with the myth of sole responsibility, his conviction that what happens in life depends solely on him. As we have seen, it is a heavy burden. We often feel unable to carry the burden and are always drained and tired. The sense of being burned out is always present. The feeling stems from early childhood and assumption of premature adult responsibility. There is no relief in sight. Theologically, we who feel overburdened have difficulty allowing God to be our companion. We experience God off in the distance, watching with no apparent interest in what is going on in our lives.

James carries a severe sense of responsibility. He says he knows he was called by God from his mother's womb. He came to the spiritual retreat not wanting to get out from under the burdens but simply to clarify what was happening in his life. He needed to explore the myths in his life so he could learn to balance his sense of responsibility with some downtime, a chance to relax and stop being constantly responsible. As a pastor, he feels he needs to learn to care for himself better through recreation and relaxation.

Identifying Themes

James's earliest memory involves identification with his father. His father was a pastor, and James remembers the Sunday morning drives to the church. There were four members of the family in the car. His parents were in the front seat, and he and his brother were in back. James remembers always sitting behind his father, and his brother sitting behind his mother. He enjoyed watching his father drive. He recalls that Sunday mornings and the drives to and from church were a time of sharing affection and warmth with his father. He believes that he bonded more with his father, while his brother bonded more with his mother.

Thus James identified early with his father and his ministry. He remembers taking his father's new dress shirts out of their packages and wearing them backwards to mimic the clerical collar. Riding happily behind his father and emulating him in dress laid an early foundation for his major theme of responsibility.

His birth order also influenced James's sense of responsibility. He was the first born, just after his father's divorce and remarriage to James's mother. James was told that he was born six months after his parents' wedding; even before the birth, his father questioned whether the child was his. James was told that his mother was hurt by his father's attitude, but they were able to work things out. James's father told his mother he was suspicious only because of an experience in his first marriage, and he regretted raising the question of James's paternity.

His father told James he remembered the night he was conceived, and how proud he was of his firstborn son. Consequently, both his parents told him his conception and birth experience, stories that then constituted his birth mythology and shaped James's view of the world and his place in it.

Of real significance to James was his father's excitement that his firstborn child was a boy. His father's image of men's role was very patriarchal; James believes he has inherited that view, having been taught that men are always responsible and must be leaders in life. His father believed that the firstborn was special and must be dedicated to God's service. With a dedication service, he kept his promise to give back to God the great gift given to him. Consequently, James feels his destiny to the ministry was sealed quite early.

James's role in his family of origin also reflected his birth order and birth mythology: "I am the firstborn child of the family. I have always felt that it was my responsibility to take care of my younger brother and sister. This was just something that the oldest was expected to do. As I grew older, this sometimes caused problems with my siblings. They felt that I was given extra privileges that I did not warrant because I was the oldest. Many times I have felt that my brother and sister misunderstood me. I remember them calling me 'Mr. Perfect' and 'Daddy's number one son.'"

In keeping with family tradition, James was also named after his father. He tried to act the role he thought was expected of him, at home and at school. He says the rewards for doing what was expected were great, but the punishments for not doing so were severe. James believes he is overly sensitive to what others expect of him; what he wants from life often gets pushed aside.

James sees negative consequences in doing what his parents expected of him all the time. He resented having to take care of his younger brother and later his younger sister. He became the family peacekeeper and organizer. As a result, he felt neglected and often wished he had an older sister who could take the role he had in the family. When he sought relief from the role, he found himself fenced in by his parents, especially his father. He believes his father had a great deal invested in James's fulfilling the eldest-son role in the family and thus found it very difficult whenever James rebelled.

James feels like Jacob, who was not the firstborn and tricked his father into giving him the blessing meant for Esau. James identifies with Jacob as the eldest, because receiving his own father's blessing was a curse as well. He knows he was born to be a minister; but it is a curse that he confuses God's call and his father's on his life. He says God reminds him often of the difference between a divine call and, by contrast, an earthly call and the desire to have a father's blessing.

James has developed a good understanding of the source of the theme of responsibility in his personal mythology. He also realizes the impact it has on him.

Mapping and Assessing

James's review of the major themes in his personal myth reveals that sole responsibility is a dominant theme. As he explored his personal myth, he discovered that premature adult responsibility was due to his birth order and the anxiety and pain in the early years of his parents' marriage. The first impact was feeling neglected by the significant adults in his life. He wishes he had an older sister, who could have relieved him of the adult role so that he could have a childhood.

James also believes there are positive consequences to his playing the premature adult role. It has contributed to a sense of accomplishment. It has brought respect and admiration from adults in his life. He believes he is better off now for having played the adult prematurely because it gave him a head start in becoming an adult. He wishes, however, that he could have effected a better balance between being responsible and his need to be a child.

In his assessment, James realizes that his personal myth was both growth-facilitating and growth-inhibiting. He needs to maximize the positive aspects of his personal myth while minimizing the negative.

Discernment

James believes that God has been involved in his life, helping to transform it: "No matter what has happened in my life, God has called me, and he determines the final destiny of my life." He believes that one can discern God's activity in the present by observing how God acted in the past. James identifies with biblical characters whose lives are similar to his own as a way to discern God's presence in his life.

James concludes that God's work in his life is similar to what God did in the lives of many biblical characters. He sees God working through the circumstances of his own birth and the parentified roles he has played. He sees his life as quite similar to Jacob's in that they both received their father's blessing, and he sees God's transformation of Jacob through changing his name (Genesis 32:22–30) as an example of how God was transforming him. While James did not wrestle with an angel as Jacob did, he does see God's involvement in helping him come to grips with key issues in his own life.

Making Plans

James feels the retreat exposed some themes in his life that need further attention. He has decided to approach planning for change by examining the Jacob story as a means of exploring his personal myth in the future. He wants to study how the pattern of God working in Jacob's life is similar to God working in his own. He thinks that reviewing past life-cycle events in light of the Jacob story can bring some new insights for growth. He believes that this process will uncover additional, significant themes. He has chosen as his methods journaling, meditation, and prayer. His journaling involves recording life-cycle experiences in a diary. In meditation, he reflects on the themes and issues uncovered in the journaling process. Prayer discerns what God is doing in helping him address these themes and issues.

Dominant Issues Raised

Some issues raised in his case need James's attention. At the end of the retreat, James was not ready to explore all the implications of his examination of his personal myth. First, he was not quite ready to deal with his feelings relating to being called by his family of origin as well as by God. *Either/or* questions about the call clearly provoked anxiety for him. He was not then at the point of awareness that there is no clear or absolute line separating God's call from that of the family. It is my theology that both are involved: God transforms the family-of-origin experiences into positive tools to be used in ministry. When James left the retreat, he was not at that level of self-examination.

James has not yet explored whether he had a real choice in responding to God when he was called. He accepted the call tradition without raising questions about it; he felt then that he had no choice.

Although I was reared in the same tradition, I feel there is a limited choice. It has to do with perceiving and perspective. Either we can choose to believe that God calls us and uses our innate gifts and experiences for ministry (as well as exposing new gifts and talents), or we can choose to believe that God calls us and it does not really matter what our gifts and experiences are. How we look at these two issues makes a great deal of difference. In the latter case, our identity is not confirmed at all. In the former, our identity does matter and is taken into consideration. In my theology, the wounded-healer model embraces our identity and experiences and uses them in ministry. Thus, the call confirms our true identity and does not work against it. The alternative, however, disconfirms our identity and makes God hostile to our growth and development. This is to say that our personal experiences and gifts are the stuff God uses to enable us to minister to others.

I believe it is important for James to continue with his reauthoring process. I have mentioned to him these two issues (whether the call was from God or family, and whether it embraced his personal gifts and talents) as possibilities worthy of future exploration.

Hope: Themes of Self-Sacrifice and Unlovability

Hope is white, single, and in her late thirties. As with James, she also struggles with knowing how to separate the family-of-origin influences from her call to ministry. She pastors a small church in a rural area, where she is well respected. She, too, believes that the call is something in which one has no choice, and that God ignores our gifts and experiences when calling us.

The people in the church community like Hope a great deal, but she points out that this is a bane as well as a blessing. The blessing is that they respect and accept her leadership as a woman. But they expect their minister to be self-sacrificing. They see her as all-giving and totally unselfish. She realizes that there is no real room to be herself as a result; she feels she is dying inside.

The precipitating event that led her to explore her personal mythology was the awareness that she could not continue her self-sacrifice indefinitely. Being "between a rock and a hard place," she needs to understand what she is experiencing. A spiritual retreat was just the opportunity she desired.

Identifying Themes and Subthemes

Hope says of the major themes and impact of her personal myth:

> The dominant themes of my personal mythology are that of caregiver and self-sacrifice. A subtheme is that love is always conditional and I am not worthy to receive it. One example of this is, as a little girl I grew up always having to take care of my mother, who was an alcoholic. I had to sacrifice myself at all times to care for her. I never had anyone to tend to my needs. I rarely received any love and affection. I always felt I had to prove my love towards others no matter if they returned it or not.

This pattern of self-sacrifice and unrequited love also held for others she knew: "Another example is my relationship with my sisters and peers. I am very supportive of them, but the support is not mutual. I am always giving of myself, but they hardly ever return this love and support. The day I was ordained, I invited all my family, relatives, and friends to share with me on what was a very special occasion for me. No one came except my mother and members of my church."

An important theme that was left out in Hope's examination of her personal myth is buried anger. She believes that to express it might drive others away, thus alienating a potential source of caring. Consequently, she strives to keep others near her as sources of love and hold on to them by being overly helpful. Under no circumstances does she express anger. She could only do so in relationships where she knows it is safe and does not threaten loss of the relationship.

Hope says she knows God's love for her is unconditional. However, she has not attempted to rely on God's love of her by itself. She realizes she needs supportive relationships. She often rejects love because she has learned to distrust others. Realizing she contributes to her own unhappiness, she feels it is because she has not learned to trust. Genuine love is possible in her mind, but she is not sure she would identify it if and when she encountered it.

The dominant themes of self-sacrifice and unlovability were developing as far back as Hope's earliest memory. The youngest in the birth order, she remembers following instructions from her parents, siblings, and larger family. She also remembers having to care for her mother when she was drunk. She felt controlled by others because she did what they wanted her to do.

Regarding her birth myth, Hope was told that her biological father and her mother were not married and that her biological father denied his paternity. He then left her mother. Hope knows very little about her mother's feelings of being abandoned. Her mother, however, was overjoyed at Hope's birth because the baby resembled her. Hope believes that once she was born she was genuinely welcomed into the world. When she was a baby, she feels that her experiences were very good and that a good life foundation was laid.

Her mother was very accepting of her gender and named her daughter accordingly, because she thought Hope would go on to do something great and she wanted her life to be lived in faith. Thus the expectation was that Hope would do something with her life that others in her family did not.

Hope's naming carried with it cross-generational expectations (McGoldrick, 1994). The expectation was that if she went on to be or do something great, that would redeem her extended family. Her mother, as the youngest in her own family, was given the role of family savior; Hope was, too, in the same way. Thus, her role was passed on cross-generationally; in fact, it was a legacy of the extended family to assign the role of the savior to the youngest child. Hope feels this was a major factor in her choice of ministry and why her mother came to her ordination: Hope was following the family tradition. She believes her sisters refused to come because they resented her for being chosen redeemer in the family.

Hope does not mind taking on her namesake role for the entire family. She believes this has contributed to her positive relationship with God. She likes having meaning and purpose in her life. But there is a negative side. The major drawback is her loss of self in the process. She does feel that her real self is involved in ministry, but she also realizes she needs to recover more of that authentic self.

The major role Hope has played in her family is caretaker. Because she clearly understands and resents this, a good place to begin editing her personal mythology would be to relinquish taking care of family members.

Her identification with stories also carries some themes related to how she views herself. Her favorite television show is "Sesame Street"; her favorite character is Big Bird because he is loved despite what he looks like. He always seems to find help when he himself needs it. He is a helper who makes others happy. Hope sees herself as Big Bird, but she would like to receive the love and help that he has. Her reediting of the personal myth can focus on learning how to ask for help from others and trusting others when they give her help.

Mapping and Assessing

Hope identifies the dominant theme at work in her life as self-sacrifice. As she began to assess the impact of this theme on her life and behavior, she said that she would sacrifice who she was in order to get others to love and accept her. She now realizes that such behavior leaves her vulnerable, easily exploited by others. When she feels that her needs are not important, she accepts that she does not deserve to have any of them met. One-sided relationships are the norm for her, where she is the one who gives while others take from her. It is hard for her to think that she can expect something in return. This self-sacrificing role is easily reinforced, and as a result she does not know how to accept permission from others not to sacrifice herself.

Hope's self-sacrificing stance is not conducive to growth facilitation. She realizes that she needs to find a more internalized sense of self-approval and not depend totally on outside approval.

Discernment

Hope finds the Bible and biblical characters helpful in discerning God's presence and work in her life. She identifies with the biblical children of Israel, who undertook a forty-year journey in the wilderness. It is through God's appearances before the children of Israel that she sees a glimpse of how God is working in her life. From reading this story, she sees that God's miracles happen in the midst of difficult situations. She has learned that it is unrealistic to expect that there will not be difficulties in life. She has discovered she can trust God to be present in her own wilderness experiences to provide leadership for her:

My understanding of God has been formed based on the story of Moses. This biblical story was told to me as a child in Sunday school and at home. The story of Moses is chronicled in Exodus, Leviticus, and Numbers, and it has had a significant impact on my life and ministry. Just like Moses, who from the day he was born was chosen by God to lead the Israelites, I feel I was born for a significant purpose in my life. Even my name proves I have a special role in life. Moses and I both have had to sacrifice ourselves on behalf of others. God loved Moses, and no matter what he faced God was present.

Hope believes that if she remains faithful to God, God will make her life meaningful. She trusts and believes that the outcome of her life will be similar to Moses'. Even though he did not reach the promised land, God guided him through the wilderness.

Making Plans

Hope created a plan: (1) to choose and read Scriptures that emphasize God's love and forgiveness, (2) to learn to accept the love of others, (3) to give up overfunctioning because it is really a need to control others, (4) to stop making herself responsible for everybody's well-being, (5) to learn to allow God to fix things, rather than her fixing things, and (6) to join a spiritual group where she can receive support in achieving her goals.

Hope's Call

She describes her call this way:

I first became aware of my call to preach after speaking at an afternoon service at church. One of the mothers of the church took me aside and told me I was going to make a good preacher one day. After a few years had passed, I acknowledged and accepted my call to preach. It was after much personal anguish, pain, and suffering that I yielded. I believe once God has chosen you to do work for him, you have no choice but to answer. God has control, and if you choose not to respond to his call, there are consequences. I tried to give every excuse why I was not worthy to be called into the ministry, but God always allowed me to know anything I lacked he would provide, just like he did for Moses.

Hope links her theology (of God being in control of her life) with the theme of self-sacrifice. For her, the call to ministry locked her into the self-sacrificing mode. She then had very little awareness of a God who calls people with a strong sense of self, so she gave in to ministry feeling that she would lose her true self forever. The God who respects her identity, gifts, graces, and experiences and uses them in ministry was foreign to her. She did not then understand how she could surrender being self-centered and still become a well-developed person.

Hope's struggle is to learn to distinguish self-centeredness from developing a healthy self. Self-centeredness is self-exaltation, the centering of attention on self while pursuing one's own ends rather than God's purposes (Peters, 1994). In classical theology, elevating the self to the center of life is pride and idolatry; it is lifting of self into the sphere of the divine. Doing so means one trusts self more than God. This understanding of self-centeredness influences Hope's thinking. She was reared not to be self-centered. However, her theology prevents her from actually distinguishing between healthy self-esteem and self-centeredness.

Contemporary feminists assert that the sin of pride is more a male phenomenon than woman's reality (Hunter, 1990; Peters, 1994). They say that women's sin is not of pride but of sloth, or the sin of not being what we are called to be by God (Hunter, 1990). According to this feminist perspective, sloth is refusing to be the self for which God holds us accountable.

It is clear that Hope does not have the sin of pride. She is not self-centered in the sense of elevating herself to the level of the deity. Rather, in this perspective her sin is, if anything, that of sloth or devaluing the self God created her to be.

Theologically, a true sense of self comes when we are connected to God and we find our sense of self enhanced by the relationship. In relationship to God, we discover a self and gifts that we did not previously know. The self is neither elevated nor deflated. In relationship to God, the self is enhanced, and our true humanity is disclosed. The God who enhances the self and takes seriously our experiences and uses them in ministry is the God whom Hope does not fully know. She needs to experience God as accepting of herself and her gifts.

Hope's call to ministry, as she experienced and interpreted the call, has not been helpful in her claiming of herself. In her mind, it means further self-denial rather than self-enhancement. She needs present and future relationships where she can experience God's unconditional love, and a community where her gifts of self are respected and cultivated.

There is a good sign that Hope is beginning to experience some of God's acceptance of her, and her own acceptance of herself. She has a theology of the Holy Spirit which affirms God's unconditional acceptance. Of her experience at the retreat, she wrote: "God has given me the anointing of the Holy Spirit and His word to use as a sign of power. He loves me just as I am. He is teaching me that way to love myself and others, just as He loves me."

This last statement holds out the hope for Hope. Through continued spiritual guidance with a small group or with a spiritual director, Hope can continue to be nurtured by her understanding of the work of the Holy Spirit in her life. It is this theology that aids her in reauthoring her self-sacrificing myth. She has only begun the process of reauthoring.

Conclusion

Both James and Hope have family-of-origin issues that need to be clarified as they carry out their ministries. Both have questions about whether those issues were the impetus of their call to ministry. They also wonder whether the call has locked them into negative patterns in which they cannot exercise their personal gifts and graces.

Both have concluded that their call to the ministry is genuine, and that they can get free enough of their family-of-origin issues to do a credible job in their ministries. They have already separated themselves from those issues enough to see that they can use their true gifts; they do not have to stay confined to unhelpful conceptions of what it means to be in ministry.

From these two cases, we religious caregivers learn that our ministries can be impacted by unresolved family-of-origin issues. Clarifying such issues and addressing them means we are freer to be in ministry and less burdened down by unresolved issues. Dealing with family-of-origin issues has the potential to free us to go beyond what we learned about ministry in our original families.

8

BLANCHE AND HENRY

SEEING OUR SPOUSES FOR WHO THEY ARE

A MARITAL MYTHOLOGY is made up of ideal expectations of what we want in a mate. It also comprises ideal images of who we are ourselves as marital partners. Exploration of the different images in the marital mythology often takes place in the marital enrichment workshops that my wife and I lead, and in the marriage counseling that I do. In marital enrichment seminars, it is possible to help spouses identify the conscious ideal images they hold. Marital counseling, however, is often necessary to help each spouse identify the unconscious, or hidden, ideal images that influence their behavior.

In addition, it is possible for couples to assess and map the influence of the ideal images, discern the influence of God at work in changing those images, and begin to make plans for changing them. In marital enrichment retreats the process of change, however, can only be started. Substantive change in the ideal images takes time; it includes the examimation of experiences of the spouses that respond only to marital therapy.

In this chapter, I present a case of a couple who came to marital counseling in order to improve their relationship. They came after attending a one-day miniworkshop on marital relationships I conducted. In the miniworkshop, they had been introduced very briefly to the reauthoring process; they wanted to know more about how to improve their relationship. As their marital counseling unfolded, it became clear that what they were doing was reauthoring their ideal images of their mate, their ideal self-image as partner, and their images of the ideal marriage. The consciously held ideal images had been capably handled in their earlier marital counseling, but gradually the unconscious ideal images that each had brought to the marriage were beginning to surface. Uncovering the unconscious or hidden ideal images helped disclose the deep emotional wounds that each had sustained in the family of origin. The pain and anxiety caused by the disclosure of these images made marital counseling very volatile at times.

Unconscious ideal images of a mate are associated with the deep personal needs that each spouse brings to marriage: the need for love, affirmation, acceptance, and affection, as well as issues of becoming an authentic self. Traditional understandings of marriage and the roles of men and women often shape our conscious ideals of our mates, of ourselves as mates, and the ideal marriage. However, the unconscious ideal images are likely to remain dormant in early marriage.

The Traditional Model of Marriage

From a theoretical perspective, there are ideal-partner images, ideal images of ourselves as marital partner, and ideal-marriage images. By far, the most important one is the ideal-marriage image, because it gives focus to the other two. Marriages operate as if there is an enduring image held by each marital partner; this persistent image appears to guide everything that is done in the marriage. Its function is to enable each spouse to perceive and orient himself or herself to reality and to the social world distinctively or uniquely. Each marriage, then, seems to be organized and function according to some ideal or overarching model of what a marriage should be (Nugent and Constantine, 1988). Knowledge of the ideal-marriage image that is operating in a marriage can go a long way toward helping the partners know what factors motivate their behavior.

Marital ideal images help individual spouses construe their collective experiences as a couple. How they do so is often brought to the marriage from the family of origin. These ideal images are also influenced by culture and are easily identified in popular media ideals that people imitate.

In the marital case presented here, the model of marriage is traditional: one where sacrifice of the self is expected for the sake of the entire marital relationship (Nugent and Constantine, 1988). Balancing the individual need to be a self with the needs of the marriage is not the norm in our culture. The prevailing emphasis is on continuity and stability in the marital relationship rather than on expression of individuality for each mate. Traditional models of marriage are usually hierarchical and grounded in patriarchal authority, or the leadership of the man. Novelty and change are viewed as dangerous; family rituals are formed around key holidays and family events so as to ensure family solidarity. The images of the ideal couple are usually from the popular media, such as those that were characteristic of the 1950s and 1960s. Leadership, most often by the man, is clear although discussion about decisions takes place between the mates. Normally, one spouse, often the man, is (perhaps tacitly) given responsibility for making the final decision. Marital roles are fixed, and conformity and agreement are highly prized.

In the initial sessions with Blanche and Henry, it appeared that each of them brought a traditional marriage ideal to marriage. Each accepts this model, it appeared to me, as the norm without evaluating whether it is best for their individual needs and marital needs. Gradually, the problems each has with this ideal began to surface as the counseling proceeded. Blanche, particularly, indicates that the traditional ideal was never her ideal. She says she adopted it at the expense of her true self because she could not envision any other workable arrangement. In the beginning of counseling, Henry, too, just assumed that all marriages function according to the traditional model.

In traditional marriages, the ideal-mate images follow stereotypical roles. The wife is expected to be dependent on the husband, to care for the home base, and to ensure the emotional survival of the family. The husband is expected to be the breadwinner and take responsibility for making sure the family has what it needs to survive materially. The unique gifts that each spouse brings to the marriage are not as important as adherence to the expected traditional and stereotypical roles for each gender.

The self-image as ideal marital partner also follows traditional roles in this model. The man expects to be responsible for the family's material survival while the woman expects to take care of the emotional needs of her husband and family. As for the woman working outside the home, this is seen not so much to fulfill her professional needs as to help the man keep the family going.

As the case of Henry and Blanche unfolded before me, aspects of the traditional model of marriage became evident. It was the task of their marital counseling to clarify that model while accommodating their unique self-understandings and the viability of the model in their real marital situation.

Background Marital Information

Henry and Blanche are African Americans. They were in their sixth month of marriage at the time they came for marital counseling. Both are recent seminary graduates. Blanche has been involved in supervisory training for hospital chaplaincy, and Henry is holding onto his secular job while hoping to achieve some of the material goals he held prior to entering the ministry. Henry is thirty-one, and Blanche is twenty-eight.

Their presenting problem emerged slowly; it focused on the level of criticism between them in their marriage. The level was very high, and the marital exchanges were often heated. They are committed to each other, and they do communicate about their likes and dislikes. They do not bring others into their marital pain, but they realize they need to reduce their criticism of each other.

Blanche describes Henry as stubborn, pigheaded, and unable to apologize when wrong. His style of relating irritates and angers her greatly. What angers her most is the difficulty she has in "trying to get through to him," which, she says, "reminds me of my mother." When she feels she is not getting through, she reverts to criticism and a sense of futility.

Henry says he is intimidated by Blanche's criticism of him. Viewing criticism as a personal attack, he defends himself vigorously. Moreover, he uses emotional distancing as a strategy to control the anxiety and pain he feels when being criticized. This distancing makes matters worse, however, since it enrages Blanche and increases her criticism. Just as Henry reminds Blanche of her mother, he says Blanche reminds him of *his* mother. His mother is very critical of him and has definite expectations she wants him to fulfill. He feels he has to keep her at a distance to have some freedom from her demands.

Thus Blanche and Henry each married someone who would help them replicate aspects of their family-of-origin experience. This replication increases the level of tension between them. Just how the families of origin relate to their marital problems and their marital mythology became apparent as the process of reauthoring their marital mythology unfolded.

Identifying Ideal Images

Their ideal-mate images emerged gradually. The conscious ideal relates to the traditional model and stereotypical male and female roles; this was apparent almost from the beginning of counseling. However, the hidden or unconscious ideal-mate images were uncovered very slowly.

Henry's ideal for his mate is that she be intelligent, capable of personal growth, committed to working things through in the relationship, and willing to sacrifice for the peace of the marriage. He expects her to be attractive and gentle, emotionally present to him, capable of expressing herself (but not too aggressively), and able to accept him with his faults. He has obviously blended the traditional expectations with some expectations that his ideal mate develop a unique self.

Blanche's conscious ideal-mate expectations are that he be supportive of her growth and development, relaxed, playful and free from too much personal anxiety, capable of sharing positive feelings, able to be emotionally present, free from financial debt and employed in a well-paying job, good-looking, and able to leave work-related problems at work. It appears that Blanche also has a mixture of expectations, some of them related to the traditional male model of providing for material needs, and others related to being emotionally available (in the traditional model, male emotional availability is not a requirement).

The unconscious or hidden ideal-mate images began to surface as the marital counseling proceeded. They relate more to family-of-origin issues than cultural images. Henry's unconscious ideal arises from his need to marry someone the opposite of his mother. He says his mother was and is controlling and manipulative, so he has always protected himself from her invasive and intruding ways—especially since his father was absent from the home when he was a child. Feeling as if his mother is a "super-cop" policing his every move, he seeks ways to be free from her aggressive supervision of his life. He does this by emotionally distancing from her. He finds it hard to relax around her.

The emotional experiences of growing up with such a mother have led him to want a mate who keeps appropriate emotional distance and who is not manipulative or controlling. When Blanche exhibits any of what he calls "mother qualities," he internally panics and seeks to defend himself from what feels like his mother's intrusive surveillance. These defensive maneuvers include competitive arguing, through which he seeks to lessen anxiety by winning an argument, and emotional distancing, just as he did with his mother. The emotional distancing, however, fuels Blanche's anxiety and exacerbates her needs for an emotionally present partner.

Blanche also brings unconscious expectations to the match. Her unconscious ideal is a husband who takes major responsibility to make her happy, and to make up for the damage done to her by her own mother and father. Feeling that her mother in particular had trouble allowing her to become a self and affirm her unique gifts, Blanche expects her ideal mate to be unconditionally accepting and affirming. This expectation means supporting her individuality and her unique way of dealing with life. In the family of origin, she had to walk on eggshells and suppress her uniqueness; now she expects her mate to be uncritical, relaxed, and encouraging of her. Any expression of dissatisfaction by Henry toward her seems to show disloyalty, abandonment, and betrayal. His criticism has a devastating impact on her; it activates internalized voices of shame in Blanche that are unbearable. She expects that marriage to the right man will silence, not exacerbate, the internal voices of shame. What Blanche needs and expects unconsciously is that her mate will dispense unlimited grace.

Henry imagines himself as a partner to be someone who can provide exactly that. His mother expected the same from him, and he learned early in childhood to take on that responsibility. He learned that he was primarily responsible for his mother's happiness. His ideal self-image says he is successful in bestowing grace, but Blanche's disappointment creates dissonance between his self-image and her image of him.

In summary, Henry and Blanche have formed a marital alliance that is the opposite of the unconscious ideals of what each wants in a mate. Neither feels the other is what he or she was promised when they married. Their courtship operated on each partner convincing the other that he or she was the fulfillment of conscious and unconscious ideal-mate images. Their present disenchantment is caused by increased awareness that their ideals are inconsistent with what they have actually encountered in the wake of the wedding ceremony. Real discrepancies exist between their ideal mates and the real mates, and it appears each is replicating a family-of-origin position. What they have is a marriage with some elements of the traditional model but additional, personal expectations that do not fit it.

It has been a long process for Blanche and Henry to come to an awareness of their unconscious ideals for a mate. With them, most of the early pastoral counseling found them blaming and counterblaming the other for not being the expected ideal mate. During that stage, my goal was to help them be less critical of each other, more self-focused and not spouse-focused. The process of moving from spouse-focused to self-focused took about six months.

Mapping and Assessing and Making Plans

After six months of adjusting their vantage points, Henry and Blanche are more aware of their unconscious ideal-mate images. Moreover, they have become more aware of how the traditional expectations of marriage and of their roles in marriage are hindering their marital satisfaction.

Henry now recognizes that his ideal self-image includes the expectation that he take the responsibility to make his mate happy and make up for all of the emotional deficits his mate experienced in her family of origin. He has also begun to wonder what appropriate role he can play in contributing to Blanche's happiness. He identifies his goal as becoming more aware of what he can realistically hope to do to help without taking away her own responsibility for her happiness. In addition, he has set as a top priority learning to distinguish Blanche's realistic needs from the unrealistic needs of his mother. His recognition of how Blanche is unique and different from his mother has increased.

At about the same time that Henry was making his breakthrough in therapy, Blanche also came to realize that she needs to take more responsibility for making her own life happy. She sees that she has her own unique gifts and voice; she wants to recapture the self-confidence of her college days, when she exercised her leadership ability.

Both have also examined how their ideal-mate images and the traditional marital expectations are limiting their growth and development. They have begun to see clearly the nature of their intense marital conflict and how they need to alter their ideal images (and their more traditional ones) regarding marriage. They are making plans and commitments: first, to explore those family-of-origin dynamics that prevent them from seeing each other's real needs and unique gifts. Second, they are committing themselves to revise their thinking about marriage to include more self-liberating attitudes, with which each person becomes responsible for her or his own happiness and where the self is not sacrificed all the time for the sake of marital happiness. Third, they are committing to learn how to be more balanced in self-expression as well as to compromise for the sake of their marital relationship.

It is clear that both need to experience unconditional grace and acceptance. They recognize that without continuing experience of such acceptance, their marital lives and their ministries will be negatively affected. But they have each decided not to depend on the other exclusively for the needed sense of grace. They are instead seeking other experiences where this need can be met. They have committed to additional marital therapy as well as to workshops and training experiences that will be supportive of their need for grace.

Discerning

While reviewing his call to ministry, Henry began to rediscover God's presence in his life and in his marriage. Reconnecting with his call helps him see grace at work in the past and in the present. God's grace was concretely evident in the past in Henry's grandfather, who extended to him unconditional positive regard when his parents' marriage was going through very difficult times. In addition, Henry feels God's presence challenging him to relinquish working so hard to solve problems over which he has very little control.

Henry's call came when he was between the fifth and sixth grades. During that time, he would have long conversations with his grandfather, who was a layperson in the church and well respected for his leadership and wisdom. Blind and unable to get around on his own, his grandfather had a lot of time for Henry. He used a lot of religious language and told his grandson a lot of faith stories, which helped Henry see how God worked in people's lives. As his grandfather was reviewing his own life, Henry felt that the God his grandfather was referring to would also have a positive influence in his own life. It was at that point that Henry began to expect God to be active in his life, as in his grandfather's life. He felt God's gracious presence; it helped Henry begin thinking about giving his life to the Lord's service. When he recalls this period of time, Henry can feel anew the gracious presence of God at work in his life.

Henry also feels that God is challenging his belief that he needs to be what his wife, mother, and sister all want him to be. That notion of duty leaves him with a tremendous sense of failure and an abundance of guilt. Guilt and feelings of failure are a heavy burden that he has long carried around. He was always motivated to try to avoid their criticism and disappointment; he was very reactive. Their expectations were intimidating and left him feeling he was in bondage. As Henry explores what he feels God is doing in his life, he finds a sense of grace and acceptance from God much as he did when he talked with his grandfather. He concludes that God's grace is present for him despite his failures and shortcomings; he also senses God pushing him to surrender the need to have to make others happy. In short, he knows that he has to become more realistic about his ability to do that for others. God is leading him to let go of this unreal expectation of himself.

Blanche's call to ministry came when she was a senior in high school. The clergy couple who were pastoring the church she attended affirmed her gifts and personal leadership qualities. Since early adolescence, she had hidden her gifts and leadership qualities in order to be liked and affirmed. The couple realized this and encouraged her to express them. Expressing her true self and exercising her leadership in the congregation, she felt good about herself and about what she was doing.

She continued exercising her gifts of leadership in college. It was the period of her life in which she felt best about herself. She helped to establish numerous spiritual groups for students and made significant contributions to their lives. Following college, she went through a major crisis in which she felt her Christian walk was inconsistent with her talk. She got involved in sexual activities that she considered inconsistent with being a moral Christian. This inconsistency led to lost self-confidence. The pattern of hiding her gifts and talents resurfaced, and once again she silenced her voice and her true self. Regressing back to her precollege personality led to chronic depression; she felt she was in bondage.

During this period of crisis and depression, she met Henry. She continued hiding her gifts from him, even after marriage, and tried instead to make her life conform to the traditional image of marriage. She put her life in Henry's hands, expecting him to liberate her from bondage, and she abdicated responsibility for doing this herself. She grew more and more depressed as a result. The longer she silenced her gifts and abilities, the more desperate she felt.

Through experiences in chaplaincy training and marital counseling, Blanche began to feel her true self emerge again. The voice she had discovered in her college days, when she was encouraged by the clergy couple, began to assert itself. A new sense of being called by God surfaced. The call involved her need to reclaim her gifts and graces of leadership. She also felt that God was calling her to take more responsibility for her own happiness.

Henry's awareness that he needs to let go of being overly responsible for others' happiness and Blanche's need to take more responsibility for her own life and happiness complement each other. They both see God at work teaching them the true meaning of oneness and mutuality. Oneness does not mean losing self or merging self into the other. Rather, it means affirming the self while also committing to the growth of the other's self. They both feel free to be themselves as well as to be in relationship with the other. Understanding what it means to be liberated and to take full responsibility for themselves enables them to commit to living in ways that support each other's need to grow. God's hand is in their new awareness. They continue to cooperate with what God is doing, to further their self-growth as well as their love for each other.

Implications for Ministry

Ministry always benefits when each person in the marital dyad is mature. Here *maturity* means having a sense of self, knowing our gifts and exercising them, being able to take responsibility for our own lives, and participating in relationships with others in ways that contribute to others' growth. The longer Blanche continues giving to others her responsibility to self so that they can make her happy, and the longer Henry feels responsible for making her happy, the greater is the danger they pose to ministry. Henry will be vulnerable to overfunctioning and burnout. Blanche will be susceptible to ineffectual ministry because she will have difficulty claiming her gifts and her leadership role. The areas in which God is challenging their personal growth and helping them reauthor their personal and marital myths are the points of most direct impact upon their ministry.

Conclusion

In this chapter, we see that substantive change in marital mythology takes time and a lot of work. Blanche and Henry's story also affirms that each couple has to fashion its own ideal marriage based on its own needs and relationship experiences. Conforming to an external ideal like that of the traditional marriage may not fit a couple's needs. Both Blanche and Henry realize that the traditional model impedes their need to be individual selves and prevents them from developing. They feel God's presence in their lives, challenging them to learn to balance self-growth with the needs of their marriage. They are learning to move toward a mutual model of marriage that affirms personal growth as well as commitment to the other's growth.

Self-development also helps Blanche and Henry both to revise their ideal images of each other. As they grow individually, they no longer need the ideal to compensate for the past. As a result, they are free to be present to the real person. Moreover, their expectations of themselves as marriage partners are suffused with grace so that they can more readily accept their own limitations.

The need for grace is a major theological theme in their marriage. They look to each other for the grace they did not receive in childhood. Recalling God's gracious presence in their lives and reconnecting with it enables them to look to God for grace and to affirm God's gracious presence through others as well. Their rediscovery of grace helps them be better mediators of God's grace as well.

9

ZELDA AND DAVID

SEIZING THE IN-BETWEEN MOMENTS
WHEN CHANGE IS POSSIBLE

SPIRITUAL RENEWAL IMPLIES—and, in reality, requires—renewal of our original call to ministry. A subsequent call can come at any point in our lives. It might be while we are engaged in some spiritual pursuit, such as a retreat or pastoral counseling. Or it can be at a perfectly ordinary moment in everyday experience. Whichever the case, at such a moment our lives suddenly come into clear focus and a new awareness dawns on us. This chapter focuses on those moments in the liminal period, the in-between times when a caregiver comes to awareness of the renewing presence . . . and the process of renewing the mythologies begins.

The Myth of Self-Sufficiency: Zelda

Zelda is fifty-eight and African American. She entered ministry, from a nursing background, in her mid-forties. She felt that a spiritual stirring in her soul was leading her to ministry. At the time, she was developing her own business caring for elderly people who could remain in their homes but needed help in doing so. She decided to give it up to go to seminary. Her children were grown and had left home, and her husband gave his blessing to her pursuit of her ministry preparation.

Zelda finished seminary after three years. She did extremely well. She established a church while in seminary, and she continued to put much effort into developing it after she finished her studies. At the same time, she also did a chaplaincy internship at a nearby hospital.

During the chaplaincy, something unusual happened to Zelda. She found that she no longer had real energy as she did when younger. And she began having intensely angry thoughts. With regard to her energy, she was used to doing what she needed to do to accomplish her goals, even if it meant going without sleep or rest. In the past she had unlimited energy to work full-time, study, and be a spouse. Now she had to get more rest and be more selective in what she ate. Moreover, she discovered that she could not make herself available to others as she once had. She had to conserve her energy.

She became very resentful of the demands that her church placed upon her. She felt that people in the church were depending on her to do everything. She liked to plan, do programming, and be in charge of the programs she was developing. Because of her need to control, she grew more and more isolated from her parishioners and ended up doing most of the work. Zelda began to wonder what was going on in her life. She sought some guidance from a spiritual retreat.

Zelda's ministry mythology was that of a loner. She believed in self-sufficiency, liked being alone, and could do a lot with her time alone. An only child, she lived most of her childhood with her grandmother, who was very strict. Zelda spent most of her time being good to avoid punishment. Zelda says that her grandmother expected her to behave responsibly and do well in school; as long as she did well, her grandmother was happy with her.

Zelda remembers that she was very afraid of the physical punishment that children received at the Catholic elementary school she went to. She was raised in Jamaica, and the school officials there were very strict. She recalled classmates being whipped; such events helped her make up her mind that she was going to be good.

Because of her grandmother's age and her fear of being whipped publicly, she became an intensely good girl. However, she also chose to be a loner so that her peers would not influence her to do things that would get her into trouble. As a result, her childhood peer relationships were quite unsatisfying.

She gradually developed a belief that she was self-sufficient and did not need people. She became a leader, and people followed her. However, she would generally overfunction in her leadership roles, and the people who followed became underfunctioners and less responsible. When she married, her husband, Courtney, followed the same underfunctioner pattern. She was able to hold all of this together until she finished seminary. At that point, she discovered feelings of anger and resentment that she had never before experienced.

These were the feelings that she brought to the spiritual retreat. She could not account for why she was so angry. On hearing her story, several retreat participants responded that she had been living her life under the tyranny of fear. She had learned to be perfect in behavior to avoid her grandmother's wrath and beatings by the school teachers. Consequently, she buried her anger over being prevented from discovering her authentic self.

At midlife, Zelda could no longer control the hidden anger. She lost the energy that had kept it under wraps. The anger found its way to the surface; caught unawares and unprepared, she thought she was having a mental breakdown. Then she felt her deep resentments about being an overfunctioner and having to do for others. She realized that her church members were not carrying their own weight, and this made her even angrier. She was discovering whole new aspects of herself, and she was extremely uncomfortable.

All her life, Zelda had entered relationships only to lead and overfunction. She had never felt that she needed others for her own support and encouragement. Now she was surprised to discover that she needed others' uplift and support. She did not want to accept the realization, and she resisted.

Zelda's midlife crisis forced her to acknowledge that she had been cut off from an important part of her life. She had to come to grips with the fearful feelings and with her deep need for support and encouragement. She had to confront self-sufficiency. It was time to accept that there was a new self emerging from within.

She learned self-sufficiency growing up. The education served her well then, because she learned to rely on herself. But by midlife her needs for interdependency, support, and encouragement from others could no longer be ignored. These inner needs were a mighty river forging its way to recognition in her life.

The Reauthoring Process

Identification of Themes

We began by exploring the themes that made up her ministerial mythology. Initially, she reconnected with her call, writing, "I remember at about the age of 14–16 I went to a Catholic priest and told him I wanted to be a nun." He talked to her about it, but she says nothing significant happened at that point. She says that later, in her early forties, she had a second set of experiences. While hosting Mary Kay beauty shows in her home, she felt a need to witness to Christ. It was a low point in her life; she felt alone and needed some direction for her life. She discovered an inner compulsion to bring people out of darkness into the light, and she began to talk to her pastor about her feelings.

Her compulsion turned into a commission. Ministry became the major motivator in her life. She has been following her commission since 1982.

A major theme in her ministerial mythology is self-esteem. It is very difficult for Zelda to be herself around others. She feels she always has to conform to others' expectations in order to be loved and accepted. She would assert who she was only if there were no personal costs to pay for doing so. This led to her feeling worthwhile only when she was meeting the expectations of others.

Zelda says she puts the needs of others first, does the work that others should be doing, and gives in around authority figures. She feels trapped, and that her life is not moving in a positive direction. When she came to the spiritual retreat, she was in bondage. She was denying her negative feelings as well as her imperfections.

Mapping and Assessing

As Zelda identifies some of the themes in her life, she begins to see areas in her ministerial mythology where she is experiencing problems. The first has to do with how she handles her feelings of frustration and anger. Zelda feels she did fairly well in dealing with frustration in the past, but she believes she has achieved still greater "success" recently. In the past, she always forged ahead in spite of feeling frustrated. Now, however, she seems to get bogged down and cannot shake it off as she once did. She feels helpless and has to admit it to herself for the first time in her life.

Zelda says that in her past she learned to disapprove of religious people ever being angry. She had to deny her feelings in trying to meet other people's expectations of what it means to be a good Christian. In our spiritual retreat, she was given permission to acknowledge her angry feelings and to own them as part of who she is. She finds that permission helpful, she feels a lot better emotionally and physically, and she is less tired. She knows it took a lot of energy to deny her negative feelings.

Making Plans

During the retreat, Zelda identified areas of her ministerial mythology she wanted to address. Her plans require some therapeutic help, so she sought me out for counseling. Following the retreat, we spent a number of follow-up sessions in pastoral counseling. She is not used to dealing with her strong, negative, aggressive feelings openly, and so I felt that follow-up would make sure she did not get overwhelmed emotionally. I was not sure how deeply buried her anger was, nor how strong were her internal sanctions against it. As a professional, I felt responsible to ensure she was not left alone to negotiate new territory without spiritual and therapeutic companionship.

As it turned out, Zelda went through several months where she was very vulnerable emotionally. For a while she regressed in her developmental cycle, and some of the long-buried feelings related to family-of-origin hurts began to surface. She did not want to be interactive or responsible for work at her church; she just wanted to disengage for a while. She took a leave of absence for several months. Gradually, she got more in touch with her deep rage and was more comfortable in admitting its presence. As she became more accepting of these feelings, she grew less intimidated by the expectations of others. She felt less compulsive about overfunctioning and began to plan how to enable people within the church to exercise more leadership. She began to see her strengths and limitations better, and as the weeks went by her desire to return to church work increased. She felt freer, more like a real person. She was glad not to have to live up to the internalized images she had maintained in trying to be an effective pastor.

Liminality

In terms of liminality, Zelda needed a period of about eight weeks to disengage from work, other ministerial duties, and related activities. Her conviction about not expressing strong negative feelings was blocking any chance of renewal in God's daily call on her life. She had to reconnect the feelings that she had split off and denied, and integrate them into her personality before a renewed sense of hope for her life and ministry could emerge. Only when she got in touch with her negative side and grew less and less overfunctioning did she discover new vitality in her life and ministry.

The presence of anger and rage signal imperfection for those of us who believe we must be perfect. To admit their presence means that we are not perfect. By denying our anger, we cannot become a whole person with positive as well as negative qualities. Zelda needs time to accept a part of her self that is essential to her ministry. As long as she denies this aspect of herself, she remains one of the walking wounded. Accepting the negative dimension along with the positive aspects of herself enables her to move from the walking wounded to the ranks of the wounded healers.

Although counseling itself is a liminal period, there are special points in the process where significant things are disclosed to the counselee. For example, Zelda had a dream with sexual and angry feelings. She was anxious about dreaming of sex and violence, but after the dream she felt peace come over her. She is not sure why she should have felt peaceful, but she wonders whether it was God's grace that she was feeling then. Because of her background, sexual and angry feelings were always suppressed beneath consciousness. In the dream, however, she could not suppress the material. It mystified her how she could have such a dream and yet not feel guilty. But to feel at peace following the dream was even more confusing to her. She finally concluded that the dream was significant because she felt accepted despite what was shameful. This means, she says, that God's grace has broken through her isolation and she is accepted for who she is as a person in spite of her imperfections.

Concluding Observations About Zelda

During the liminal times of counseling and dreams, Zelda has experienced God's gracious presence at work in her life. This helps her sense that she is no longer alone in ministry and that it is a shared task involving God as well as others. Without these periods of liminality, it is doubtful that she would be in a position to alter her ministerial mythology.

The Myth of Sacrificing Joy: The Case of David

David tells how he worked a paper route and delivered groceries as a preteen to make sure his six brothers and sisters ate. His father was not involved in the family; nor did his mother have steady work because of her drinking. There were other relatives, but he says the responsibility for the family fell on him and his older brother. He tried to have fun and do the things that other children did, but he always had to give up those pleasures because of responsibilities at home. "Not only did I learn responsibility," he says, "but I learned self-discipline, determination, and unselfishness."

When he was fourteen, his mother had a serious accident and had to distribute her children among relatives. David moved to another city, separated from his brother and sisters. He says he began to thrive as a person. He had his own room for the first time. He did very well in high school and finished it. He postponed college for several years following high school but later earned his bachelor's degree. At twenty-three, he accepted Christ; he says it helped fill the void that he felt in his life. Married, he began to think about the ministry. He entered seminary, and on completion he served in the military chaplaincy while raising three children. Close to forty when he left the military, he entered parish ministry. It was at this point that he came to our spiritual retreat.

In the parish ministry, there was some conflict with parishioners who felt he was too tense and emotionally unavailable to them. They said he tried to be too bossy and always seemed to be rushed. They found him too uptight and in need of relaxing more.

Identification of Ministry Themes and Subthemes

When he began to explore his ministry mythology at the retreat, David commenced talking about his childhood responsibility: "As a child, I learned responsibility early. In being responsible, I had a tendency to want to control and assert my own agenda on others. In my relationship to congregations, I came with a lot of ideas and therefore attempted to change the worship services and the people to what I thought best. I was controlling, so I often found myself in conflict with them. I soon discovered that this was a mistake. However, I found my salvation when I was able to enroll in CPE during the time of conflict."

He says the CPE experience taught him things that helped him overcome some of what he brought into adulthood from childhood. The major thing he has learned is to relinquish control whenever he is anxious and in the midst of conflict. What helps him, he says, is the input, support, and encouragement he receives from supervisors and peers to sit with his anxiety and allow things over which he has little control to surface in the church. Learning to be less anxious has taught him a very important lesson: the more maturely he handles his own anxiety in conflict situations, the more level-headed people in the congregation are mobilized to help resolve the conflict. Without learning this, he would continue trying to keep conflict under his feeble control.

In the retreat, David admitted he was having difficulty with his teenage son. He was irritated at the boy for enjoying life, and David resented that. He kept "lifting up" before his son the need to be responsible and to make something of his life. He now feels he is resentful of his son because David lost a great portion of his own childhood and adolescence through the unfortunate circumstances of that period of his life.

Mapping and Assessing

During the retreat, David explored the themes in his personal, marital, family, and ministerial mythologies. Notable are the themes related to overfunctioning, ideal expectations for his children, his need to be in control when there is conflict, and his inability to relax and enjoy life. He has committed to discover what he enjoys doing and to make sure he does something that he likes several times a week.

David's inability to have joy, along with his overfunctioning in ministry, came from childhood experiences and premature adult responsibility for the family when his mother was unable to function. In ministry, he found an opportunity to continue playing this overfunctioning role; however, playing the role has caused him conflict with parishioners uncomfortable at his need to control. He now has to confront his way of relating and functioning in his ministry and in his family. He has to confront the themes in his various mythologies and revise them.

Period of Liminality

Revisiting his call as part of the reauthoring process, David reveals that entering the ministry was a process and was nothing remarkable. He brought to the retreat a dream through which he got in touch with an important dynamic. The retreat was a significant time of liminality for David; his inner life was more accessible, largely because his small group within the retreat was so supportive. His dreams became a source of nurture and new meaning for reinterpreting his life.

He dreamed of a house with a baby in it. The baby was in a crib, and a dog was threatening the child. Frightened, it tried to climb out of the crib. David saw what the child was doing and picked it up. The dog continued its harassment, and a group of men in turn began to harass David and the baby. But he ignored them; he reported that he was not frightened, only concerned. The scene in the dream shifted: an angel appeared, singing, "He is worthy." David told his group it was a male voice, but very high pitched. The dream ended.

The group members were much drawn to the dream and immediately began helping David explore its meaning. They first asked what David thought it meant in terms of his life. He felt the dream had to do with the circumstances of his present life and what he was facing in his church and family. Real stresses, internal and external, were threatening him; the dog and the men symbolized those threats and stresses. Although he knew he had very little control over them, in the dream there was a significant change within him. Forces in his life, which in the dream were represented by the dog and the men, used to subdue him, such that he would feel they had him in prison. They were so menacing that he dared not contravene them to be himself. Now, with this dream, he felt a change had taken place; the major threats were no longer fearful, no longer held him in prison. The appearance of the angel was the welcomed presence of God, showing him he was no longer alone in facing destructive forces. He identified the angel as God's protective presence, which would accompany him in dealing with life's threats. He said the angel brought considerable peace to him.

The group members helped David explore the significance of the baby. Some were aware that images and characters in a dream often represent aspects of the dreamer's own personality. Babies often symbolize the presence of a vulnerable child who has not been nurtured into adulthood and needs protection as well as support to grow. This made sense to David. The interpretation helped him think of the vulnerable child in him, the child who stopped growing and developing in order to care for an alcoholic mother. The frightened child within inhibited his ability to enjoy life. From the angel and his own nurturing image in the dream, David saw that this child no longer had to fear danger; it was time for the child to grow.

The spiritual retreat, the time spent in his small group, and his attending to dream material constituted a liminal period for David. He had been struggling for years in his family and church, wanting to come to grips with his concerns. He had come to the retreat desirous of reauthoring his entire belief system.

David's new understanding of his life came from several sources. The first was within himself: his own experience. Second, he had knowledge, biblical and psychological, about the function of dreams. Third, through clinical pastoral education he had struggled with some of these issues himself. Fourth, his group members were well versed and sophisticated enough in the psychology and spirituality of dream symbolism and interpretation to be of help. Fifth, the retreat itself was geared toward understanding spiritual renewal as an ongoing connection with God's presence as it unfolded in one's life through daily renewal of the call. As a consequence of these sources of understanding, we can see that—not only for David but for all of us—exploration of ministerial mythology and dreams in the context of a spiritual retreat encourages bringing our life experience into line with what God is doing in our lives to bring renewal of purpose.

Spiritual consciousness is a private matter; it is often experienced alone, or with a spiritual director. The themes of self-sufficiency and individualism contribute to keeping the process of spiritual renewal a solitary one. This often exacerbates the loneliness and isolation of ministry. We have been reminded, however, that ministry is not a solo activity, nor is spiritual renewal exclusively a solitary experience. Rather, spiritual renewal can take place as well in small groups; this is the significance of a spiritual retreat offering a relational context for the reauthoring process, as was true for David. In such a context, spiritual renewal is communal, involving processes of story telling, story listening, story linking, and story transforming. It also makes use of Scripture, religious images and symbolism, psychology, dream interpretation, and the company of spiritual companions and guides (McKenner, 1995).

Making Plans

David feels he made significant strides during the retreat. There are, however, some unresolved issues that he needs to address. His new insights and intended behavior in relationship to them will be enhanced if he spends some time in personal therapy, working on consolidating the gains made at the retreat. We always fear that the enthusiasm of a retreat will soon wear off, as the reality of unfinished personal business in our lives resurfaces. David has decided to make sure he follows up on getting assistance with his growth through therapy.

Conclusion

Liminality is an important period for religious caregivers. It can be intentional, as when we recall memorable experiences that can nurture us in the present. Or it can be spontaneous, where something suddenly marches onto the stage of our lives and discloses new, life-changing insights. Whether sudden and dramatic or intentionally used for reflection, liminality is an indispensable stage in the spiritual renewal of religious caregivers.

10

FROM WALKING WOUNDED TO WOUNDED HEALER

WHAT TO EXPECT ON THE JOURNEY

THIS BOOK INTRODUCES A MODEL for reauthoring our personal, marital, family, and ministry myths. The components of the model extend back to Scripture and to the African American "call tradition." No doubt, remembering our call as a means of spiritual renewal is a universal and natural dimension of any faith tradition where the oral style of communication is dominant. As we turn to the final insights about the reauthoring model, I offer some further comments about the importance of renewing our call as religious caregivers by way of recalling our stories.

Within two weeks of writing this final chapter, I had an opportunity to lead a group of ministers through the reauthoring process. They came together to find better ways of relating to each other as peers in the same denomination. Most of them had been working in their parishes, in isolation from each other and from other peers within and outside their denomination. They had been suffering the pains of isolation in silence and had decided to do something about their seclusion. The group convened to address their separation at the urging of the women pastors, who not only sensed the loneliness of detachment but also felt themselves dying emotionally and spiritually as a result. The men sensed the isolation as well, but they were generally more used to denying their need for peer partnership. The pastors organized their group and called me, asking if I would help them address their lack of working and peer relationships. We set aside a weekend for a spiritual renewal retreat, where they could work together on their concerns.

I have suggested that returning to our call and our stories is an important means of decreasing the distance and fostering bonding among ministers (and other religious caregivers). This combined resource of recalling in the presence of others and completing the mythology questionnaire (the exercises at the end of Chapters Two through Four) lowers the barriers that keep us from relating to each other. The group of ministers examined not only their lacking relationship with each other but also their relationships with family members. They also explored their present work situations. The spiritual renewal weekend had some exciting outcomes:

1. The airing of distrusts and grievances that existed among them
2. Correcting misconceptions and attitudes that existed among them based on isolation and rumors
3. The beginning of bonding between them, which they so desperately needed and desired
4. Progress in discerning God's presence in their local parishes
5. A renewed sense of hope for overcoming isolation
6. A renewed sense of vocation grounded in revisiting their original motivation for ministry

In addition to this, many of them found exploring their myths to be interesting and insightful as to why they were doing some of the things they were doing. Some of them made a covenant to continue exploring their myths together as a means of deepening their newfound relationships.

In this chapter I offer a few examples of what spiritual renewal looks and feels like when it follows upon the reauthoring process. Vignettes focus on the impact of the process on people's ministries and their lives. I then address selected issues that reauthoring raises for religious caregivers. Finally, I make some comments about each step in reauthoring.

The Rest of the Story

Reauthoring as a process unfolds step by step over a period of time. It is grounded in returning to our call to ministry and examining our myths in light of the ongoing call on our lives. Reauthoring starts a lifelong endeavor that passes through periods of in-depth exploration. The examples I share here are reports of a reauthoring process in progress; they are not intended to be a final summation of the reauthoring process.

Zelda: No Longer the Loner

Zelda is the African American woman caregiver (from Chapter Nine) who did her work in isolation, believing that she was sufficient unto herself to carry out the work of the church. Suffering from fatigue, exhaustion, and isolation, she almost reached a psychotic break from reality. She was handling uncontrollable rage that had festered for years, stemming from early childhood experiences that largely shaped her mythologies.

After taking a four-month sabbatical leave, in which she engaged in pastoral counseling and reauthoring of her various myths, she decided to return to her parish work with new knowledge of how her myths have undermined her ministry. She has decided not to be a loner any longer. She is developing a lay leadership program so that she will not go on doing everything herself. Discovering what it is like to be in partnership with others in ministry is scary for her, but she remembers the pain of what it was like to be alone. She says she would rather suffer uncomfortable feelings than return to the hell of being isolated. She is also surprised at her new level of energy and hope for her ministry and her life.

David

Another reauthoring success is David. His myth of sacrificing joy (which we also looked at in the preceding chapter) prevented him from enjoying his family and made his parishioners uncomfortable being around him. He was too domineering in the church and people were generally afraid of working with him.

David spent six months in pastoral counseling attending to his myth. He has made a real effort to learn to relax and play. The crowning achievement for him was to buy season tickets to a local NFL team. Pro football is one form of permission to himself to have some of the fun he never had as a youth while caring for an alcoholic mother. His children and parishioners find that he is now much more pleasant to be around. The programming at the church now centers more around fellowship and celebration than just business matters. He is loosening up. He no longer sees play as trivial or a waste of "good" time.

James and Hope: Discovering New Gifts

An unanticipated result of people engaging in the reauthoring process is the discovery that some have talents for specialized ministries rather than ministry in general. Several persons who have spent time in pastoral counseling attending to their myths have developed an interest in working with others in "depth pastoral counseling" and have decided to develop their skills and gifts in pastoral counseling training to augment their ministries. Some have also discovered gifts in the area of conflict resolution and have sought training in this area. Others found a renewed interest in theological education and are seeking to enter Doctor of Ministry programs.

For many, reauthoring has led to unanticipated benefits. This is the case with the two people we discussed in Chapter Seven. James discovered he had a deepened interest in working with others in spiritual formation and began to seek specialized training. Hope desired to develop support groups for pastors and began to work toward that end.

Douglas: They Don't All Live Happily Ever After

Not all reauthorings have successful endings. It would be easy to report only the positive outcomes; but it is important to suggest the very different results that are possible as well.

I think of one case where the caregiver was so deeply wounded that he was prevented from reauthoring his marital mythology. Douglas had suffered at the hands of a punitive father and siblings and an emotionally unavailable mother; he turned to marriage as his way of finding healing for his wounds. He had ideal expectations of a spouse able to heal him, but—as we might have predicted—instead he married someone who actually replicated his family-of-origin experience. He was unable to foresee how he would seek a marital role for himself—and choose someone who would help him—to stay in the familiarity of abuse. In spite of a year of pastoral counseling, he still blamed his wife for all his problems.

The sad lesson in Douglas's outcome is that myths are often resistant to change. They hold on, just like the demon who is cast out but returns with many friends. It is important to point out that the joys of reauthoring come as the result of painful personal work. Not all pain can be worked through; not all outcomes of reauthoring are positive.

Key Issues

Engaging in the reauthoring process raises some key issues that need full exploration. Here we briefly address several of them.

Realism

Part of the problem with not-so-successful cases such as Douglas's is the theological perspective with which the caregiver approaches reauthoring. While reauthoring is possible, an appropriate theology is needed to shore up the total process so that we as caregivers do not develop a false sense of confidence in undertaking it and become overly optimistic about its possibilities. A fellow pilgrim in the reauthoring process makes an instructive comment about the significance of an appropriate theological outlook:

> My story has a positive plot in it, despite the fact that it had the sacrifice of myself at the center. Despite the fact that I had to sacrifice myself to be loved by others, I can see that God was at work in my life helping me to come to grips with what it was like to live in the Wilderness. The Wilderness is the place where we have to come to grips with our negative stories and to dedicate ourselves to what God is doing to bring our ultimate freedom. The Wilderness is not easy, but it is essential to our growth and development. It is in the Wilderness that we confront our inner selves and our idolatrous myths.

For this reauthorer, the process of crossing the wilderness teaches how to let go of the security blanket. In reauthoring, we learn to trust God's gracious leading of us—with a cloud by day and a fire by night. She sees that we have to let go of our internalized beliefs about ourselves, to see ourselves and our experiences the way God sees us. She adds, "I had to accept the fact that human love is conditional, but God loves me unconditionally." Her comment is significant because she is not elevating the need for love from others to the center of her life and leaving God out. No, she is working on not sacrificing *herself* to win love. She recognizes that God loves her regardless of self-sacrifice. The love she experiences from God at work in her life during the reauthoring process frees her to accept her unique gifts of self and to offer them to others without apology.

This theology is realistic about life. Hers is a wilderness theology, not a triumphalist one. Her wilderness understanding of theology is based on what happened to the children of Israel in the desert, and how they took forty years to learn what it meant to trust God amid pain and suffering. They could not treat suffering trivially; they had to take it seriously. Triumphalism is a theology that either trivializes suffering or denies its influence in life. An appropriate theology for reauthoring takes suffering and evil seriously and finds God's presence and work in the midst of it all. Such realism about the presence of suffering and evil helps us trust the unfolding of the spiritual renewal process that God is leading. It helps us not try to control or predict the outcome. It forces us to trust the outcome of our renewing to God.

Companionship

Another issue is the isolation of religious caregivers. As with ministry more broadly, reauthoring is not a place to go it alone. I don't recommend that you do the reauthoring by yourself, for a number of reasons. It is not good spiritual self-care to do so. It can be risky emotionally and spiritually. Rather, I encourage you to covenant with a small group of trusted peers, a spiritual guide or director, or a counselor or therapist. Have someone to whom you can turn in the process of reauthoring. I emphasize that reauthoring myths should be thought of as altering the basic structure that heavily influences your identity, your self-esteem, your way of being and relating to the world and others, and your orientation to life. Seeking to modify the tried and recommended approach could be a risk-taking enterprise; I hope you will not enter it unadvisedly or without companionship.

Those of us who feel we have a good sense of self apart from others and have been working on family-of-origin issues for a long period with some success can engage in this reauthoring process with peer support. However, if you are just beginning to work on family-of-origin issues and are struggling with developing a sense of self apart from others, it is important to have professional guidance available from an experienced spiritual guide or therapist.

Getting the Most from the Exercises

By reading this book, you have essentially already begun the reauthoring process. You may also have completed some of the exercises. The question remains: How do you derive the most from the end-of-chapter exercises for your renewal? I now draw on responses from those who have engaged in the reauthoring process to help you get the most out of using the questionnaire exercises in Chapters Two through Four.

Many people who have used the exercises find that naming their myth helps them immensely in the reauthoring process. Naming enables you to form a mental image or picture of your myth; this can give focus to what you are doing. Some choose a TV show to provide a mental picture or name for their myth. We can understand how family myths might attract naming from popular TV families: "Family Ties," "Leave It to Beaver," "Ozzie and Harriet," and "The Cosby Show." Other caregivers identify with specific characters in plays, movies, or the Bible as a means of helping them to name their myth:

I have compared my story to Hansel and Gretel, saying that, "It is the journey from the cage or furnace home to uncover the answer to the question why." Just as Hansel and Gretel were able to use bread crumbs to find their way back home, we too through the process of self-discovery can uncover "bread crumbs" which can lead us to inner healing.

The story of Hansel and Gretel is a fitting one for me to use, for there is a sense that I was like them in that my life has been a sense of trappedness or helplessness (i.e., being caged). However, my sense of being trapped usually stems from feeling trapped between things rather than by things.

This person used the "Hansel and Gretel" story to understand what was going on in his reauthoring process; it gave him hope and comfort as a result of naming an aspect of his myth. While feeling caught "between" others, he found the crumbs that led him out of being caught.

Some people name their myth by focusing on the kind of plot behind it. Distinguishing whether the plot is positive or negative in direction helps to focus the reauthoring. Negative plots head toward pessimistic outcomes, while positive plots head toward constructive outcomes despite the obstacles. Those who see positive plots at work in their lives do not avoid suffering or pain; they see God at work amid travail and distress.

Helping caregivers identify alternative stories while reauthoring is another important tool. As we begin to use the exercises and identify the themes and their impact on our lives, we may also encounter buried stories we have lived that hold out potential for renewing our lives. Exploring these stories for their possibilities is an important dimension of dealing with renewal while reauthoring.

Some find alternative stories by identifying with biblical characters. The figure of Moses was particularly helpful to one caregiver in her reauthoring process. She reflects on her own call in light of Moses' call:

Moses, in the third and fourth chapters of Exodus, objects to his calling because he does not have the ability, a message, the authority, the eloquence, or the inclination. Moses felt unworthy to be called to ministry. He was not perfect in his own mind. In fact, this was the heart of his protest about being called.

I felt the same way when I was called to the ministry. I thought that I would make some big mistake and not be perfect. I wanted to be a perfect child, and I blamed myself for not being good enough for ministry. Now, I realize that God called Moses not because of his perfection, but because of his humanness and despite his flaws. This was true for me also.

Through identification with Moses, she finds the grace needed for her to embrace the call. Thus identification with characters in the Bible, or in literature or real life, helps us reauthor negative myths.

I suggest a final way to get the most out of the reauthoring process: avail yourself of feedback from others. As our peers listen to us, things get stirred up in them. Often, what is stirred up is of great benefit for our own growth and development. Consequently, hearing what others experience as we recall our own stories is important to our reauthoring.

Reauthoring Is Always in Order

Recalling our own stories as we seek to be renewed is always in order. We need periodically to reconnect with our original motivation for entering the ministry, to bring focus and perspective into our lives. There are times, however, when we ought to engage in reauthoring for the sake of our own souls and those of others.

When we hit a brick wall in our ministry or personal lives and are having an extremely difficult time handling things we once were able to do with ease, it's time for reauthoring. Often, our rigid myths are blocking our ability to respond to certain situations and problems. For example, I thought that my wife and I were mature enough bring my aging parents to live with us. Little did I realize how totally unprepared we both were for this undertaking. If I had not confronted my perfectionistic self-image, I would not have been able to deal with the new situation. I would have been unprepared to handle my parents' being in our home with the old myths of myself. I had to revise my self-mythology quickly; given the circumstances, I had no choice. Indeed, most new situations in life are an opening for modifying our mythologies.

The Steps in Reauthoring

As we move systematically through the steps of the reauthoring process, problems arise at each point that might need attention.

The Questionnaire and Identification of the Myths

For example, in writing out the exercises of the mythology questionnaire so as to identify the themes that are at work in our personal myths, we may encounter emotional pain in the section on birth mythologies. This is especially the case if we sense we were unwanted and unloved. In doing certain exercises, there is always the possibility that painful memories and experiences might be triggered. This is reason enough for not engaging in the renewal process alone.

The assessment sections of the mythology questionnaire may also cause us to pause as we try to pull all the information into a consistent perception, image, or mythology. Tracing cross-generational themes in the personal mythology section is particularly crucial; it may appear to be a nonconstructive or growth-debilitating task. Discovering a pejorative cross-generational legacy might be too much for us to handle at the time. Here again, companionship is essential as we attempt to forge a wholly new perspective of our lives. It can be scary to traverse this terrain alone. Moreover, we may see additional revelations as we get feedback from others.

Mapping the Influences of the Myths

Mapping the influence of the myths on our lives may not be as difficult as identifying them. Yet, here too, things could be missed if we do this step alone. Generally, I believe that those who do this step diligently—that is, with the willingness to have others feed back information or simply to have them accompany and support us—find it very helpful in discovering just how certain themes have shaped their lives.

Discerning God's Presence

As each successive step in the reauthoring process assumes the center stage of our attention and concentration, the process gets harder. The third stage of the reauthoring process, discerning God's presence, brings us liberation and affirmation, yet it too can be anxiety provoking. Trying to cooperate with what God is doing can be difficult for many reasons. We might not agree with what God is doing even though we know it will benefit us. Second, we might feel that *we* have a better idea of what God could be doing for us. Third, we might find it hard to discern or hear what God is actually doing. Finally, knowing neither the future nor the final outcome of the reauthoring process, we might resist God's leading in our lives. These feelings and resistances are normal, and the best prevention of such anxieties and concerns is to have companionship along the way. There is no substitute for the caring of others as we attempt to negotiate the wilderness way. Overcoming our tendency to go it alone is one of the benefits of learning to reauthor our myths.

Making Plans

Making plans to edit our myths is not always easy. Knowing what is influencing our lives in negative ways and deciding to alter it is often difficult. We are likely to resist making plans and then following through with them. It is important to have some kind of companionship to help us get through the periods of resistance. We may be willing, but it is not easy to let go of certain life patterns and beliefs that we are very familiar with.

Conclusion

There will be many moments in our lives when we will have the opportunity to reauthor our myths. These opportunities are part of God's creation, and of God's continued presence and work in renewing our lives as well as creation itself. God's way of working in our lives is very much like the unfolding of a book: it proceeds one chapter at a time. Recalling our own stories as a process, one step at a time, is a good way to renew our lives as religious caregivers.

REFERENCES

Achtemeier, P. J. *Harper's Bible Dictionary.* San Francisco: Harper San Francisco, 1985.

Bagarozzi, D. A., and Anderson, S. A. *Personal, Marital, and Family Myths: Theoretical Formulations and Clinical Strategies.* New York: Norton, 1989.

Berger, P. L., and Luckman, T. *The Social Construction of Reality: A Treatise in the Sociology of Knowledge.* New York: Doubleday, 1966.

Bowen, M. *Family Therapy in Clinical Practice.* Northvale, N.J.: Aronson, 1978.

Clinebell, H. *Basic Types of Pastoral Counseling.* Nashville, Tenn.: Abingdon Press, 1984.

Corey, G. *Theory and Practice of Counseling and Psychotherapy.* Pacific Grove, Calif.: Brooks/Cole, 1991.

Doehring, C. *Taking Care: Monitoring Power Dynamics and Relational Boundaries in Pastoral Care and Counseling.* Nashville, Tenn.: Abingdon Press, 1995.

Erickson, B. M. *Helping Men Change: The Role of Female Therapist.* Thousand Oaks, Calif.: Sage Publications, 1993.

Fenn, R. *The Dream of the Perfect Act: An Inquiry into the Gate of Religion in a Secular World.* London/New York: Tavistock, 1987.

Fiorenza, E. S. *In Memory of Her: A Feminist Reconstruction of Christian Origins.* New York: Crossroad, 1992.

Framo, J. "Symptoms from a Family Transactional Viewpoint." In C. J. Sager and H. S. Kaplan (eds.), *Progress in Group and Family Therapy.* New York: Brunner/Mazel, 1972.

Friedman, E. H. *Generation to Generation: Family Process in Church and Synagogue.* New York: Guilford Press, 1985.

Gabbard, G. O. *Psychodynamic Psychiatry in Clinical Practice: The DSM-IV Edition.* Washington, D.C.: American Psychiatry Press, 1994.

Gill-Austern, B. "Love Understood as Self-Sacrifice and Self-Denial: What Does It Do to Women?" In J. S. Moessner (ed.), *Through the Eyes of Women: Insights for Pastoral Care.* Minneapolis: Fortress Press, 1996.

Glover-Wetherington, M. A. "Pastoral Care and Counseling with Women Entering Ministry." In J. S. Moessner (ed.), *Through the Eyes of*

Women: Insights for Pastoral Care. Minneapolis, Minn.: Fortress Press, 1996.

Guerin, P. J., Fay, L. F., Burden, S. L., and Kautto, J. G. *Evaluation and Treatment of Marital Conflict.* New York: Basic Books, 1987.

Hollifield, E. B. *A History of Pastoral Care in America: From Salvation to Self-Realization.* Nashville, Tenn.: Abingdon Press, 1983.

Hunter, R. *Dictionary of Pastoral Care and Counseling.* Nashville, Tenn.: Abingdon Press, 1990.

Interpreter's Dictionary of the Bible. Vol. 2. Nashville, Tenn.: Abingdon Press, 1993.

Jewett, R. *Saint Paul at the Movies: The Apostle's Dialogue with American Culture.* Louisville, Ky.: Westminster John Knox, 1993.

Jewett, R., and Lawrence, J. S. *The American Monomyth.* Lanham, Md.: University Press of America, 1988.

Jordan, M. R. *Taking on the Gods: The Task of Pastoral Counseling.* Nashville, Tenn.: Abingdon Press, 1985.

Jung, C. G. *Modern Man in Search of Soul.* Orlando, Fla.: Harcourt Brace, 1933.

Kerr, M. D., and Bowen, M. *Family Evaluation: An Approach Based on Bowen Theory.* New York: Norton, 1988.

Klagsbrun, F. *Married People: Staying Together in the Age of Divorce.* New York: Bantam Books, 1985.

Mace, D., and Mace, V. *What's Happening to Clergy Marriages.* Nashville, Tenn.: Abingdon Press, 1980.

Malony, H. N., and Hunt, R. A. *The Psychology of Clergy.* Harrisburg, Pa.: Morehouse, 1991.

May, H. G. and B. M. Metzger (eds.), *The New Oxford Annotated Bible with the Apocrypha, revised standard version.* New York: Oxford University Press, 1977.

May, R. *Power and Innocence: A Search for the Sources of Violence.* New York: Norton, 1972.

McGoldrick, M. *You Can Go Home Again.* New York: Norton, 1994.

McKenner, M. *Angels Unawares.* Maryknoll, N.Y.: Orbis, 1995.

Messer, D. E. *Contemporary Images of Christian Ministry.* Nashville, Tenn.: Abingdon Press, 1989.

Miller-Mclemore, B. J. "Women Who Work and Love: Caught Between Cultures." In M. Glaz and J. S. Moessner (eds.), *Women in Travail and Transition: A New Pastoral Care.* Minneapolis: Fortress Press, 1991.

Moessner, J. S. "A New Pastoral Paradigm and Practice." In M. Glaz and J. S. Moessner (eds.), *Women in Travail and Transition: A New Pastoral Care.* Minneapolis: Fortress Press, 1991.

Moessner, J. S., and Glaz, M. "The Psychology of Women and Pastoral Care." In M. Glaz and J. S. Moessner (eds.), *Women in Travail and Transition: A New Pastoral Care*. Minneapolis: Fortress Press, 1991.

Myers, W. H. *God's Yes Was Louder than My No: Rethinking African American Call to Ministry*. Grand Rapids, Mich.: William B. Eerdmans, 1994.

Neuger, C. C. "Women's Depression: Lives at Risk." In M. Glaz and J. S. Moessner (eds.), *Women in Travail and Transition: A New Pastoral Care*. Minneapolis: Fortress Press, 1991.

Nichols, M. P. *Family Therapy: Concepts and Methods*. New York: Gardner Press, 1984.

Nichols, W. C., and Everett, C. A. *Systemic Family Therapy: An Integrative Approach*. New York: Guilford, 1986.

Nouwen, H. *The Wounded Healer*. New York: Doubleday, 1972.

Nugent, M. D., and Constantine, L. L. "Marital Paradigms: Compatibility, Treatment, and Outcome in Marital Therapy." *Journal of Marital and Family Therapy*, 1988, 14(4), 351–369.

Oliver, W. *The Violent Social World of Black Men*. San Francisco: New Lexington Press, 1994.

Passmore, J. *The Perfectibility of Man*. London: Gerald Duckworth, 1970.

Patton, J. *Is Human Forgiveness Possible?* Nashville, Tenn.: Abingdon Press, 1985.

Peters, T. *Sin: Radical Evil in Soul and Society*. Grand Rapids, Mich.: William B. Eerdmans, 1994.

Phelps, J. "Black Spirituality." In R. Maas and G. O'Donnell (eds.), *Spiritual Traditions for the Contemporary Church*. Nashville, Tenn.: Abingdon Press, 1990.

Pillari, V. *Pathways to Family Myths*. New York: Brunner/Mazel, 1986.

Poggi, G. *Calvinism and the Capitalist Spirit: Max Weber's Protestant Ethic*. Amherst: University of Massachusetts Press, 1983.

Poling, J. N. *Deliver Us from Evil: Resisting Racial and Gender Oppression*. Minneapolis, Minn.: Fortress Press, 1996.

Rediger, G. L. "A Primer on Pastoral Spirituality." *The Clergy Journal*, Jan. 1996, pp. 17–20.

Richardson, A., and Bowden, J. (eds.). *The Westminster Dictionary of Christian Theology*. Philadelphia: Westminster Press, 1983.

Rizzuto, A. *The Birth of the Living God*. Chicago: University of Chicago Press, 1979.

Satir, V. *Conjoint Family Therapy*. Palo Alto, Calif.: Science and Behavior Books, 1967.

Satir, V. *People Making*. Palo Alto, Calif.: Science and Behavior Books, 1972.

Snorton, T. E. "The Legacy of the African-American Matriarch: New Perspectives for Pastoral Care." In J. S. Moessner (ed.), *Through the Eyes of Women: Insights for Pastoral Care.* Minneapolis, Minn.: Fortress Press, 1996.

Taylor, J. M., Gilligan, C., and Sullivan, A. M. *Between Voice and Silence: Women and Girls, Race, and Relationship.* Cambridge: Harvard University Press, 1995.

Van Kaam, A. *Religion and Personality.* Garden City, N.Y.: Image Books, 1964.

White, M., and Epston, D. *Narrative Means to Therapeutic Ends.* New York: Norton, 1990.

Wimberly, A. S. (ed.). *Honoring African American Elders: A Ministry in the Soul Community.* San Francisco: Jossey-Bass, 1997.

Wimberly, A. S., and Wimberly, E. P. *One Household One Hope: Building Ethnic Minority Clergy Support Systems.* Nashville, Tenn.: Division of Ordained Ministry, United Methodist Church, n.d.

Wimberly, E. P., and Wimberly, A. S. *Liberation and Human Wholeness: The Conversion Experiences of Black People in Slavery and Freedom.* Nashville, Tenn.: Abingdon Press, 1986.

INDEX

A

Abuse: and good girl myth, 24; and sense of powerlessness, 20, 21; and underfunctioning, 68–69
Acceptance: and grace, 119, 122, 137; of personal identity, 106, 111–112
Achtemeier, P. J., 101
Acts 25:13–26:32, 2–3
Affection, myth of unlimited, 45–46
African American spirituality, model of spiritual renewal in, 3
African Americans: good girl myth among, 23–24; matriarch image among, 64; sense of powerlessness in, 19; womanist images among, 64
Agrippa, King, 2–3
Aloofness myth, 27–28; and self-sufficiency myth, 63
Anderson, S. A., 15, 16, 36, 37, 78
Anger, buried, 107–108, 124–125; acceptance of, 126–128
Anxiety: and conflict, 129; in reauthoring process, 77, 78, 85, 140–142
Assessment. *See* Mapping and assessing
Attributions, 74, 75
Attunement, 7. *See also* Empathy
Authority, 60
Authority Exercise, 71

B

Bagarozzi, D. A., 15, 16, 36, 37, 78
Berger, P. L., 74

Birth mythologies: and call to ministry, 103; in examples, 93, 103, 108; emotional responses to, 141; in family mythology, 49; in ministerial mythology, 62; in personal mythology, 17–18, 21, 26–27
Birth Mythology Exercise, 30, 78
Birth order, 90, 93, 103, 108
Birth Order Exercise, 30; in examples, 93, 103
Boundaries: in caregiver relationships, 53; in family of origin, 27–28, 68
Bowden, J., 101
Bowen, M., 60
Burden, S. L., 36, 83
Burnout: and negative myths, 35; and pleasing others, 68; and sole responsibility myth, 25; and spiritual renewal, 1, 4

C

Call Exercise, 70
Call to ministry: biblical tradition of, 11–13, 101; divine versus family-of-origin sources of, 101–112; examining the sources of, in personal mythology, 101–112; narrative story and, 5; and personal identity, 106, 111–112; as project of existence, 4; reconnecting with, 1–4, 5, 88, 100; reconnecting with, in case examples, 101–112, 119–121, 123–132; reconnecting with, in community of colleagues,

3, 133–134; problem of perfection and, 6–9; sacrificing joy and, 128–132; self-sacrifice and, 110–112; self-sufficiency and, 123–128; sole responsibility and, 102–106; women and, 11–12; wounded healers and, 11–13, 106

Calvinism, 65–66

Capitalism, 65

Caregivers: bonding among, 134; "three families of," 38, 53. *See also* Ministerial myths; Ministry

Catastrophic expectations, 67

Challenge, and envisioning transformation, 75–76

Change, first versus second order, 82. *See also* Transformation

Childhood, loss of, 38–39. *See also* Premature adult responsibility

Childhood experiences, 15; and origin of personal myths, 15, 17. *See also* Family of origin

Cinderella, 44

Clinebell, H., 6

Clinical pastoral education (CPE), and vulnerability, 8–9, 24, 129

Closeness: and myth of aloofness, 27–28; and myth of the loner, 21–22

Cognitive narrative structures, 35–38

Columbus, C., 75–76

Columbus risk, 75–76

Community of colleagues, reviewing call to ministry with, 3, 133–134

Constantine, L. L., 114

Contraction phase, 49

Corey, G., 67

Counseling, need for, versus retreat model of reauthoring, 83–84, 126–127. *See also* Marital counseling; Pastoral counseling

Crisis, and transformation, 75, 86–88, 124–125

Cross-generational expectations, 108

Cross-generational themes, 141

D

Damascus Road, 2–3

Dire consequences myth, 51–52, 54

Discernment stage: difficulties in, 141; of reauthoring marital myths, 119–121; of reauthoring ministerial myths, 85–86; of reauthoring personal myths, 80, 96–97, 105, 109–110. *See also* Liminality

Disciple role, moving to steward role from, 88

Discipline Exercise, 31; in example, 94–95

Dissociation, 98

Divorce and remarriage, symbolic, 82

Doehring, C., 7, 13, 68

Dreams, 128, 130–131

Dual relationships, 53

E

Earliest Memory Exercise, 29, 78; in examples, 92, 103, 108

Emotional investment, 38

Empathy: childhood experience of, 16; "good enough," 8; myth of perfect, 6–8

Entitlement myth, 69

Environment for reauthoring, 77

Epston, D., 73, 76, 79

Erickson, B. M., 23, 24–25

Everett, C. A., 82

Exercises: Authority Exercise, 71; Birth Mythology Exercise, 30, 78; Birth Order Exercise, 30, 93, 103; Call Exercise, 70; dealing with difficulties in, 140–142; Earliest Memory Exercise, 29, 78; Gender and Sex Exercise, 30; getting the most from, 138–140; Ideal-Child Image Exercise, 56; Ideal-Family Image Exercise, 56; Ideal Mate/Marriage Image Exercise, 56; Ideal-Parent Image Exercise, 56–57; in